The Twists & Turns of Possibility:

My Life is My True Story

Principal Michael McGrone Sr.

November Media Publishing, Chicago IL.
Copyright © 2018 Principal Michael McGrone Sr.

All rights reserved. No part of this publication may be reproduced, distributed, or transmitted in any form or by any means, including photocopying, recording, or other electronic or mechanical methods, without the prior written permission of the publisher, except in the case of brief quotations embodied in critical reviews and certain other noncommercial uses permitted by copyright law. For permission requests, write to the publisher, addressed "Attention: Permissions Coordinator," at the email address below.

November Media Publishing info@novembermediapublishing.com

Ordering Information: Special discounts are available on quantity purchases by corporations, associations, and others. For details, contact the publisher at the email address above.

Printed in the United States of America

Produced & Published by November Media Publishing

ISBN: 978-1-7326897-3-2

First Edition : September 2018

10 9 8 7 6 5 4 3 2 1

TABLE OF CONTENTS

Chapter 1: In the Beginning 1

Chapter 2: Finding My Place 23

Chapter 3: Dino 31

Chapter 4: The Death of Superman 43

Chapter 5: College Material 50

Chapter 6: A Dream Deferred 66

Chapter 7: Love Prelude 76

Chapter 8: McGrone the Renegade 81

Chapter 9: Rites of Passage 97

Chapter 10: Paying the Price 108

Chapter 11: The Road Ahead 125

A word from the author...

My parents, Charles and Rosetta McGrone, lived complex lives. They never got a chance to go to college and live out their dreams. They both came from large, fractured families and were victims of a perpetual cycle of violence and dysfunction. The impact of their childhood experiences had devastating implications on the way they reared my siblings and I. Though they relied upon God for strength and guidance, for a long time I resented the way I was raised. Only now do I realize that God gave me the perfect parents to prepare me for His purpose, which is to use me to restore hope, rebuild dreams and save lives. My parents did the best they could with what they knew, and I can never repay them for the sacrifices they made. My goal is to live a life that honors them by fulfilling God's purpose for my life. I now realize that the person I am is the result of the values they instilled within me as a child. I am the outward sign of their inner peace. My hope is that the social emotional trauma "thrivers" who read this book will gain a greater understanding of life and all its complexities. But, more importantly, I hope they will understand that real success comes by way of pain – the greater the struggle, the greater the achievement. See you on the other side. Peace and blessings.

ACKNOWLEDGMENTS

I would first like to thank God for his grace and mercy on my life. I've faced death several times, and I have often been lost and angry; but with His guidance, I have found my place in this vast world. I would like to thank my parents, Charles Edgar McGrone (deceased) and Rossetta McGrone Santokie. Because of their prayers and devotion to God, I am living a life worthy of their pride. To my siblings: through it all, we've managed to fight through the pain, stay connected, and keep each other strong. I would like to thank Mrs. Fisher, my 5th grade teacher, for empowering a kid with low self-esteem to feel like he belonged. I would also like to thank the mentors who each stepped into my life at the perfect time to play a critical role in my life's journey. They believed in me, poured energy and time into my life, and gave me the courage to stand on my own. Their unselfish ways changed the trajectory of my life and gave me a new outlook. I would like to thank the mother of my children, Eileen, for providing a loving and nurturing environment for our family while I was all over the place trying to "save the world". I would like to thank my children, Mike Jr., Jeremiah and Anaiah; they give my life meaning and a sense of purpose. They are the sole reason I eventually returned to school and graduated. I didn't want them to experience the emotional trauma that I endured as a child. They are now well-balanced and growing up to be exceptional children. They are the light of my life and I love them with all of my heart. I would like to thank Debra Johnson-Givens. She never lost faith in me and remained by my side. I am grateful for her selflessness. She is one in a million and has a heart of gold. Lastly, I would like to thank Rodney Walker who ultimately became my mentor after my time mentoring him. Rodney inspired me to write this book. The late-night talks, the questioning, the tears and the pain ran deep, but somehow, we made it through. Because of him, the world will have an opportunity to know my story. He has become more than a "mentee"; he has become my best friend. I am proud to have been his best man on the day he was married.

Rodney Walker and me getting ready for his wedding.

DEDICATION

To my children

Chapter 1

IN THE BEGINNING

Gary, Indiana was once known for having one of the largest steel industries in the world. During that time, you could graduate from high school and still earn a living to take care of your family. Downtown Gary was bustling with businesses and entertainment for its citizens. Homes were beautiful and well-manicured. Though segregation still ruled parts of the city, it was nonetheless a great place to live. Gary had a growing population of African Americans that had reached well over 50% in the late 60's. Politically, African Americans were gaining popularity due to the civil rights movement, and in 1968 they would vote for the state of Indiana's first African American Mayor, Richard G. Hatcher. It was a joyous occasion; however, it would mark the beginning of the end of an era. This didn't sit well with many of the white residents as they started to move south of Gary to areas like Crown Point, Portage, Merriville, and Schererville. When they left, they took resources with them, which profoundly impacted the city in a devastating way. Homes would be left vacant for years to come and become havens for drug addicts. Many times, dead bodies would be discovered in them. Downtown Gary, once beautiful and decadent, would become a ghost town, a mere shell of its former glory. Schools were closing at a record pace, taking with them all of the city's history (**Note:** Literally every school I attended is now closed). The unemployment rate ballooned out of control and as a result, residents left the city in droves to find work and a better way of life. Gary's prominent past would become a distant memory and have devastating implications in the years to come.

In November of 1966, my Aunt Mag introduced her brother, Charles McGrone Jr., to my mother, Rossetta Meux. They would get married in Chicago only after dating for two months. My grandmother, "Mu," would play an intricate role in their courtship because she thought Charles was a good fit for my mother's personality. My father was patient, but my mother, on the other hand, was a pistol. She was incredibly feisty! My mother had one son, Dino, at the age of 16; my father, divorced from a prior marriage, had 7 children. My mother was unaware that my father had 7 children and would temporarily leave him for several months. This put a strain on my father; he was devastated. He worked hard to earn back my mother's trust. Eventually, they would end up together. As the years progressed, the complexities of a blended family would cause significant challenges.

My mother suffered from depression which my father was ill-prepared to deal with because of his own feelings of inadequacy. My mother was dark-skinned and hated the complexion of her skin. She was considered the problem child – the black sheep of the family. She was tough, though, and wore it like a badge of honor. She would tell us stories of how she would fight grown men. My mother knew she had mental health issues and once tried to check herself into a mental institution; however, she never did. Her fear was that the state would see her as an unfit mother and take her children away; as a result, she never got the help that she desperately needed. My father was a quiet man. He rarely got angry unless provoked. He stood 6'2" and weighed over 300 pounds. His fair complexion validated my mother's existence because of her insecurities and lack of self-worth.

On May 12, 1970, my mother gave birth to my twin sister and me on her birthday, which was coincidentally also on Mother's Day. Until the moments following Michelle's birth, the doctors were unaware that my mother was carrying two children. She arrived five minutes ahead of me and reminds me quite often who's the oldest. As you can imagine, I was quite a surprise. I was the first boy born to the union of my parents.

At the time, I had three older siblings: Dino, Kim and Tammie. We came from the hospital to a one-level, three-bedroom home with only one bathroom. My childhood home was literally the size of a garage. After the birth of Michelle and I, my father quit his job as a butcher and got a job at Industrial Pneumatics where he repaired tools for the local steel mill. In the following years, my parents would go on to have five more children together (Rodney, Jamie, Roxanne, Kenyon and Lori). My father worked long hours to support us, from 6 A.M. to 6 P.M. When he came home, he smelled like he had bathed in motor oil. He was always tired, but he made time to play with us. I remember jumping on his back as he let us ride him around like a horse. He would also take his unshaven face and rub it up against ours. The hairs felt like little spikes, but we loved it. He would squeeze our jaws with his fingers, and though he never verbally said "I love you," we knew that it was his own way of expressing his love for us. My siblings and I still do it to each other in remembrance of him.

My first childhood home, 1029 Stevenson St. in Gary, Indiana

My mother made sure we loved and respected him because of the sacrifices he made to take care of us. When he returned home from a hard day's work, we treated him like a king. We had his favorite meal ready: smothered chicken and gravy with white rice, and a cold glass of ice water.

Once he was done eating, we'd run his bath water, so he could take a warm, relaxing bath. Each of us would take turns washing his feet and scratching his scalp, all while he watched "Sanford & Son," one of his favorite TV shows. He also loved watching wrestling with characters like "Dick the Bruiser," "Rick Flair," "Andre the Giant," and "The Claw." We would all pack into his room to watch T.V. with him. We enjoyed taking care of him.

Back then, he made only $500.00 every two weeks. As you can imagine, it was not enough to support a family of our size. Our grocery bill alone was over $1,200.00 a month. My mother had to rely on food stamps to adequately take care of us. We also frequented the local food pantries to help ends meet. I recall going grocery shopping with my mother, and it was definitely hard work. We would literally have several buggies overflowing with food. No one ever got behind us at the check-out line. Despite the hard work, I loved going shopping because my mother always allowed whoever went with her to pick out their favorite cereal. My favorite cereal was King Vitamin (a generic brand of Captain Crunch).

My mother was never formally diagnosed with a mental illness, but she suffered from the symptoms of depression and bulimia. She would go into intense rages that would frighten the heck out of us. Her eyes would become bloodshot and she would have the most evil look on her face. It was as if she were possessed. When she went into these manic episodes, she would bite down on the inside of her right jaw, pull her hair out, punch herself in the face, and strip naked in front of us. She would also cry and scream uncontrollably as she ran through the house, breaking anything that she could get her hands on. She dumped buckets of water and trash throughout the house . She damaged appliances. Every time she had these episodes, my siblings and I would start cleaning the house as quick as we could, mopping, sweeping and picking up the trash she had strewn throughout the house. Somehow we thought that cleaning the house would make matters better; however, these episodes would go on for hours at a time. This had a profound effect on my social emotional development and academic performance. I began to lack self-confidence and internalized my feelings. I always wondered if my father knew about my mother's intense rages. I wanted him to protect us. Incidents typically happened in the morning right before I got ready for school. I was not able to focus and I didn't trust anyone at school to tell them what was going on. I was afraid of what would happen to me if I did. At times, I would catch myself daydreaming in class, wondering what mood my mother would be in once I returned home. We never knew what to expect. My mother could be kind one minute, and then in a split second, become our worst nightmare.

One incident that is forever etched into my mind took place when I was about six years old. I stole some food from the kitchen to share with my brother Jamie because we were hungry. Momma chased me into the bedroom I shared with my two younger brothers. I crawled under the bed. She screamed for me to come out from under the bed but I refused. My fear of her was very visceral because when you got a spanking she made you strip naked, get into a tub of water, and then she would beat you with an extension cord. I can still remember the pain to this very day.

Knowing that this was my reality, I refused to come out from under the bed. This infuriated her, so she went into the kitchen, tore up a brown paper bag and lit it on fire. She came back into the room and crawled underneath the bed, as far as she could, pointing the flames at me. I backed myself into the far corner to escape the flames. All I remember is the intense heat, fire, and smoke coming toward me. I started choking and coughing; I was terrified! I surrendered and got the worst whooping. The beating lasted until she got tired. I had welts all over my body. That single incident would have a lasting effect on how I felt about my mother. I never liked being in the same room with her. I became numb to the beatings, so she became even more sadistic. In one incident, she grabbed my hand and started biting my fingers. I thought she was crazy. I still wear the scars to this day. I had no idea at the time that my mother suffered from mental illness and needed professional help. Since she was afraid of seeking psychiatric help, she relied on prayer to be her saving grace, which meant she would never get the aid she desperately needed. As a result, my siblings and I had to endure the physical and verbal abuse for years on end. I know that my mother loved us, but because of her own demons and feeling of incompetence, she had an extremely difficult time showing it.

Nevertheless, my mother bonded with us through music. She had the most beautiful voice, and would sing to us often. She played the piano and was the lead singer in the church choir we attended. My siblings and I would inherit her gift of musicality. Today, all of us can play an instrument, sing, or both.

The Cost of Growing Up in Gary

The 80's drug epidemic infiltrated the streets of Gary and ultimately had a devastating impact on entire communities. My friends and other folks I knew began to use drugs and exploit the drug trade for their own economic gain. Some even became big-time drug dealers. I remember seeing my friends drive around in expensive cars, wearing expensive jewelry and the latest designer clothes. They also were feared and had a lot of power and control. In my mind, they were living the good life. My mother didn't want us to get caught up in the drug game, so she became even more aggressive in her parenting style to keep us off the streets. I recall one incident when I went to play basketball at Jackson Park off of 4th Avenue. It was a park where drug dealers and gangs regularly hung out. She warned me to stay away from the park; however, I decided to disobey her wishes. As I was playing an intense game of basketball with my friends, I noticed my mother suddenly pull up in an old grey Pontiac. It was especially embarrassing because the car had rust spots and the paint was peeling. She rushed out of the car with a broom in hand. It was one of those heavy-duty industrial brooms. She chased me around the park, hitting me everywhere she could. She connected a few times, but I acted like it didn't hurt; however, I was in excruciating pain. There was no way I was going to cry in front of my friends. The whole ordeal was humiliating, and my friends made fun of me. I was the brunt of everyone's jokes. Needless to say, it would be quite some time before I returned to the park. I despised my mother's unorthodox parenting style; however, in hindsight, she was saving my life. So many of my friends died as a result of being drug dealers and gang members.

Living in a community where violence was commonplace had a devastating effect on me. I began to normalize death. It became commonplace because it happened so often. I also heard the sound of gunshots and people arguing every day, especially at night. To cope with the unwanted noise, I slept with a fan to drown out the sound (for most of my adult life, I couldn't sleep without one). However, the noise that I despised most came from my room that I occupied in the basement.

The neighborhood I lived in was infested with rats and roaches. Rats dug holes alongside the house and made their way into my room. I could hear them claw and squeal throughout the night. I slept with the cover tightly tucked under me, fearing they would crawl on top of me. When I would turn the lights on, I would see them scatter back to where they came from. As you could imagine, I hated turning on the lights. I would brace myself from what I knew to be obvious. The roaches were terrible, too. They were everywhere. They especially infiltrated the kitchen. At times, they made their way into the refrigerator and got into food that was not secured in containers. They thrived in the darkness and when the lights were turned on, they too would scatter.

One of my most embarrassing memories came when I was in high school and a roach crawled out of my book bag. My classmates went crazy; however, they had no idea that it came from my book bag. I acted like I was surprised, too. To this day I can't stand the sight of a roach. More importantly, I can't stomach seeing food in a refrigerator that is not secured in a container. Since I associate filth with rodents, I've become a bit of a neat freak. I will never live in a house with rodents again! I truly appreciate the stillness of the night. I no longer have to worry about gunshots and rodents keeping me up at all hours.

At the age of 10, I witnessed an older man get killed right in front of me. I was running home after watching a house go up in flames. When I got to the corner of 5th and Jackson, I saw him walking across the street, carrying a six-pack of beer. I then saw several men hanging outside the window of what appeared to be a sky-blue Cadillac with sawed-off shotguns. They were parked in the alley alongside the liquor store where the man came from. Their eyes were fixed on him the whole time. Soon thereafter, gunshots rang out. My heart was racing and I couldn't move. Everything happened so fast. I was scared because I had made eye contact with the shooters and I thought they would come after me; however, they sped off. I saw the unidentified man land headfirst, making a loud thump.

After the coast was clear, I ran over to his body. For a brief moment, I was motionless as I stared over him. I could still see gun smoke coming from his body and blood pouring from seemingly everywhere. I was scared to death and was trying to process what had just happened. I closed my eyes, said a prayer, and ran home as quickly as I could. I told my mother what I had witnessed; however, she didn't believe me. Her response to me was to go and lay down. As you could imagine, I couldn't sleep. I was traumatized. I thought the incident was over. However, the next day when I went to school, I noticed my teacher consoling one of my classmates, Angelique. She told the teacher how her uncle was murdered on the corner of 5th and Jackson in explicit detail. I overheard the conversation and was in utter shock! She had no idea that I witnessed the entire incident. I was so frightened and scared that I never said a word. I kept telling myself that one day I was going to tell her what happened. However, it wouldn't happen until 37 years later, when I found Angelique on Facebook and told her to call me. I was nervous because I didn't know how she would react. When she called me, I told her everything and how sorry I was for what happened to her family member. I told her I saw him take his last breath and that I said a prayer for him. I explained to her the reasoning it took so long for me to talk about the event; I told her I had suppressed it for years (especially because my mother didn't believe me) because it was so traumatic. I tried to make it disappear, but the memories were too vivid to let it go. This unidentified man would become part of my everyday life. I never forgot him. As I explained to her what happened that night, she was surprisingly calm and told me that she had moved on years earlier. She said that the matter was resolved years ago, though it was still fresh in my mind. I told her that I carried that nightmare with me for years.

I asked her for the name of the man, because for years he had been a nameless figure to me. I felt spiritually connected to him because I saw him take his last breath. She told me his name was Ricky and was adamant that I knew his son who was named after him. She sent me pictures of the unidentified man and all of the memories came rushing back, as if I were reliving the entire incident. I remember that day as if were yesterday; he had a perfectly-shaped afro and long sideburns, even as he lay lifeless. When she sent me pictures of his son, I was blown away. She was right; I had known his son for years. He went to Horace Mann High School with my siblings. He was a really good athlete, and very competitive. We even played football against each other. That moment changed my life forever. I didn't see life as so innocent anymore. I had a hard time understanding what happened and became desensitized to anything that made me feel emotional or physical pain. In essence, I learned at a young age how to internalize my feelings. I became my own worst enemy. I sabotaged relationships and dealt with matters alone, even though I had a support system. Through prayer, counsel, and education, I have now become more expressive and vocal about my feelings. I am no longer afraid to be vulnerable. I'm grateful to God that I was finally able to close that difficult chapter in my life and move on.

Open Door Church. The church I attended in my childhood.

Religion played a critical role in the way I was raised. We attended numerous churches; however, the church that made the greatest impact in my life was called the Open-Door Church. The Open-Door Church was a full gospel congregation, where they believed there was, "Nothing right but holiness." When you entered the church lobby, there was a window case filled with prescription medication, canes, corrective shoes, wheelchairs, neck braces, etc. The idea was that churchgoers were being healed from years of physical and emotional abnormalities. At a young age, I didn't believe in miracles because although my mother was prayed for countless times to heal her depression, her behavior never changed; in fact, it had only gotten worse. My mother took a natural problem and made it spiritual. The tendency to do this is pervasive in the black community. It goes undiscussed, enabling us to refuse to seek the help we desperately need. My goal is to bring awareness to mental health issues in our community in an effort to prevent other children from enduring experiences similar to those I faced.

Furthermore, I was afraid every time the pastor made an altar call. During this time if you were a "sinner" it meant "giving your life to God" and "confessing your sins." He explained that if you were not "saved" and God came back, you would burn in a lake of fire forever and ever. Needless to say, I was "saved" every Sunday or any time I went to church. I didn't want to take a chance of going to hell. I had nightmares about going to hell all of the time as a young man.

My father was the deacon and drove the church bus. He was a fiery preacher. I enjoyed watching him preach "The word". He played the lead guitar, too. My mother was the lead singer in the choir, and my Aunt Cynthia played the organ. I felt proud seeing my mother sing. She would get everyone involved in praise and worship and she prepared the congregation to receive the pastor's lecture.

Going to church several times a week and staying there for hours at a time made me resent going to services. It was a restrictive environment. You couldn't listen to secular music and the women were not allowed to wear pants or make-up. Everyone referred to each other as Sister so-and-so and Brother so-and-so. The church doctrine did not believe in sparing the rod, either, so my parents felt justified in whooping us, "in the name of Jesus." They called it "beating the hell out of you." The measures used to correct our behavior were borderline sadistic, but the church saw nothing wrong with them.

The women in the church also seemed to show more affection towards the pastor than to their husbands. I had a problem with that because I was taught that no one came before my father... he was the king.

Though my mother suffered from mental illness, she always prayed over my siblings and me. She would walk throughout the house, praying in the middle of the night, putting "blessed oil" on our foreheads. She asked God for favor over our lives and for Him to protect us. This happened throughout my childhood, despite her explosive episodes. She also would fast often in the name of religion (go without eating) for weeks at a time. It was her way of battling depression and sacrificing her life to preserve the lives of my siblings and me.

My Reality

From 1969 to 1978, as I mentioned earlier, we lived in a three-bedroom home. With a growing family of twelve, we were bursting at the seams. So, in November of 1978, we moved to 413

We moved to 413 Madison Street in 1978

Principal Michael McGrone Sr.

Madison Street. The couple we bought the house from was named Mr. and Mrs. White. They were an elderly couple and would be one of the last white folks to move from a neighborhood that was growing more and more diverse. The house was beautiful and well-kept. It looked like a mansion in comparison to the house we moved from on Stevenson Street. I remember when we first moved in, Jamie (6 years old) and I were sleeping on the living room floor, and he started crying, saying, "This house is too big… this house is too big."

I put my arms around him and reassured him that everything would be okay. The fact of the matter was that the house still had three bedrooms and one bathroom. The only difference was that it had a large living room, basement, and upstairs area. The basement was one big large open space, so my father sectioned it off to make room for additional bedrooms. My brothers Rodney, Jamie and I slept in a twin-size bed; Dino, my oldest brother, set up his bedroom next to the furnace. The bed Rodney, Jamie and I slept on was in poor condition and had pee stains everywhere. The springs were broken and would protrude from the mattress and cut into our skin. I would stuff the holes with old socks to prevent them from cutting into us. We were kids, Rodney hated getting up to use the bathroom and would wet the bed. His urine would get all over me, and we would end up fighting in the middle of the night. At one point, my mother made him sleep with plastic underneath him so that he would not continue to soak the mattress. Since we slept opposite from each other, Rodney's feet would always end up in my face. This would infuriate me so much that we would jockey for the best sleep position in the middle of the night. Because Jamie was younger, he hung off the bed. Though Rodney and I had our battles, we nevertheless had a close relationship. He was wise beyond his years. We had deep discussions in the middle of the night about life. Later on, I could call Rodney in the wee hours of the night and he would respond on the first attempt. To this day, he is still a wise old soul.

The block I grew up on was fun. Our neighbors would place their house speakers out on the front porch and blast the latest hits. We would dance our butts off. I can still remember listening to the sounds of Earth, Wind & Fire, the Isley Brothers, Stevie Wonder, Marvin Gaye, Bootsy, Parliament-Funkadelic, and other soulful artists. The block parties were amazing! Everyone would cook their favorite dishes, set up camp and socialize with each other. It was a day filled with fun activities. There were several large families that lived on my block and we all played together. We would compete against other neighborhoods in basketball and football. We won most of the time and took great pride in that we had the best athletes. We were good!

We called ourselves the "5th Ave. Boys." We fought each other but were always friends again the next day. The neighborhood kids went to the local boy's club. Though it was called the boys club, the girls were allowed to go, too. I learned how to play pool and won numerous trophies and awards. I won my first spelling bee contest at the boy's club. I can still remember like it was yesterday. I won spelling the word "watermelon." My siblings and I not only went to the boys club for the extracurricular activities, but also because they fed us well. Food was scarce at home so we took advantage of the free meals there. The staff was really nice, and it was a place to feel safe and enjoy ourselves.

I rarely smiled because I had inherited the McGrone gap and I always felt self-conscious. However, an incident happened when I was in the 2nd grade that would stop me from smiling for years to come. I was in the hall right outside the cafeteria at Ivanhoe Elementary School, lining up to go back to class, when an upperclassman shoved me into the concrete wall. The impact cracked my two front teeth. I was rushed to the nurse's office as blood spurted everywhere. I was spitting out pieces of my teeth. The pain was excruciating. Any time my teeth were exposed to the air, it would send shock waves through my body. I had to learn how to eat using the side of my mouth. My parents did not have insurance, so I would endure the pain and ridicule for years. I did not get my teeth fixed until I was in the 8th grade. There was no way I was going to junior high school looking like that. I had been bullied all through school and I was ready to close that chapter. When I was fourteen years old, my mother gave me the medical card and I took myself to the dentist's office on the second floor of the bank building on 5th and Broadway. Though I got my teeth fixed, I still felt apprehensive about smiling. It took me years to feel comfortable smiling again.

Academically, I was never a strong student. I failed the 3rd grade. The day everyone got their report card, they were excited because they would move on to the 4th grade. My report card indicated that I had to repeat the 3rd grade. I remember like it was yesterday, and I was devastated. Everybody was showing off their report cards, and I was too embarrassed to show mine to anyone. Ms. Evans was my 3rd grade teacher and all I can remember is how cruelly she treated me. I never felt like she cared about me. Being retained had a devastating effect on my self-esteem. All of my friends, including my twin sister, moved on to the 4th grade. What compounded the problem was that Kindergarten through 3rd grade students ate lunch during the first period, while the 4th through 6th grade students ate during the second period. This meant I would continue to eat lunch during the first period. I remember lining up across from my friends on the ramp to go back to class and them making fun of me. I completely shut down. I felt shame and embarrassment. This was the beginning of the end of a potentially joyous childhood. From that moment on, I became what people's perception of me was... a failure.

The ramp at Jefferson elementary to line up to go back to class

The next year, I repeated the 3rd grade with Ms. Comer. She was really nice and soft-spoken. I was at my lowest and rarely spoke, but she made me feel safe. One night I got a really bad whooping with a leather belt. My brother Dino had just been released from jail and I wanted to see him; however, my parents warned me to stay away from him. He was staying at a transitional facility (halfway house), so I snuck out to see him. My parents found out and came to pick me up in an old white two-door pick-up truck. I knew I was in big trouble. When I got home, I tried to prepare myself as best I could by putting on layers of clothes. My mother was angry that I defied her authority and provoked my father into whooping me. My father was really strong so he beat me by holding me upside down while he held my feet together. He only stopped when he got tired. I had welts all over my body. When I went to school the next day it was really hot; however, I wore a long sleeve thermal shirt to school to cover the marks on my arms and torso. The welts were so bad that the dried-up blood stuck to my shirt. I wanted Ms. Comer to ask me why I wore a long sleeve thermal shirt on such a hot day, but she never did. Had she asked me, I would have told her everything. As an educator, I vow to never overlook the obvious. My goal is to protect my students at all cost, even if it means turning in their own family members. I can spot a victim of abuse a mile away because of my own experiences.

To learn from my past, I had to learn how to discipline my own children without resorting to extreme measures of violence. I didn't want them to endure the physical and emotional scars I had lived through. I began working on myself to understand what my triggers were. My goal was not to repeat history. I've learned how to talk to my children and incorporate other disciplinary measures without breaking their spirits.

The teachers at Jefferson Elementary School were strict. Most of them lived in the community and knew our parents. This made it difficult to get away with anything. During that time, corporal punishment was allowed. My 4th grade teacher, Ms. Brayboy, was tough. She had high expectations and was a true disciplinarian. If you acted out in her class, she dealt with you herself. She never sent you to the principal's office. She had several rulers she had taped together and if you would misbehave she would make you hold your hand out and smack you until it turned red. Needless to say, I rarely had any disciplinary problems in her class. She had high expectations and pushed you to be great. She made me love math. I would go to the chalkboard to write out my answers and if I got the problem right she gave me a donut.

Mr. Williams was the principal, and when I got in trouble I always ended up in his office. He was tall and thin and wore an afro. He always smelled like a pack of cigarettes but nonetheless he knew how to use the paddle. Not only that, but he had a unique way of paddling you. He made you start off doing push-ups and would rest the paddle on your behind. I would always look back to brace myself to minimize the pain. He would always say, "Don't look at me son." After about three swats, you learned to stay out of trouble early on.

Mrs. Fisher

In 5th grade, I had a serious crush on Mrs. Fisher. She was the most beautiful woman I had ever met. She always called on me to read first. I was also her number one classroom helper (at least, that's what I thought). She often asked me to erase the chalkboard after class. To me, it was another opportunity she wanted to spend time with me. I really thought she wanted to be my girlfriend. One day she invited me to church. I was so excited! We were going on our first "date." I dressed in my Sunday's best. When I arrived, I noticed that she had a pretty white dress on. The church was packed with guests. She looked beautiful; however, to my surprise, she had invited me to a ceremony to renew her

Me with Mrs. Fisher at Thea Bowman H.S. in Gary after keynote address

vows with her husband. I was devastated and called my mother to pick me up. I was angry with her for a long time and didn't want to be her classroom helper anymore. I can laugh about it today; however, I was serious about our "relationship" back then. She had no idea the depth of my feelings for her. With everything that was going on in my life, she made me feel safe and valued. To my surprise, she treated everyone with the same love and compassion. The attention she gave me is something that I desperately yearned for. I couldn't wait to get to her class so that she could water my soul. In 2016, I got an opportunity to tell her the whole story and she thought it was hilarious. I admitted to her that she broke my heart; I just knew we were going to get married. I later told her that the day she renewed her vows was the day that I broke up with her. Mrs. Fisher and I are good friends to this day and she continues to inspire me. She was my angel on earth during a dark time.

In 1984, my parents allowed my twin sister and I to move to Cincinnati to stay with my Aunt Barbara. My parents were contemplating moving there. My Aunt Cathy and cousins from Gary also moved in. Aunt Barbara had a full house. My twin sister and I attended Merry Middle Junior High School. It was one of the worst school experiences in my life. I didn't have any friends. I was bullied quite often and was the brunt of everyone's jokes because I wore hand-me-down clothes. One day, I wore a green army suit to school I bought from a rummage sale. The lady who I bought the army suit from had a husband who was a veteran who recently passed away, and she was selling his belongings. I thought I looked sharp (I always liked dressing in suits). I became the laughingstock of the school. I was chased home by a group of boys as they threw apples at me from a nearby orchard tree. In another incident, I got suspended from school for fighting in the middle of an assembly. The student who was sitting behind me kept kicking my chair and I warned him several times to stop, but he continued. I told the teacher but she refused to do anything about it, and he continued kicking the back of my seat. So, right there in the packed assembly, I got up and punched him in the face and we started fighting. I got suspended, of course. Aunt Barbara was furious because my complaint fell on deaf ears. The following day, I returned to the school with my aunt. She wanted to question the principal regarding my suspension; however, the principal was not changing her mind. My aunt cussed her out and had to be escorted out of the building. She was not a woman to be trifled with. She was a beast! My time in Cincinnati was short-lived. I hated it. I felt out of place. Though my aunt was very nice, I missed my family. I begged my father to come get Michelle and I. After much convincing, my parents packed up the entire family and they hit the road. I was so happy to see everyone and even more happy that I was returning home.

Upon my return to Gary, I realized that the city was hit hard by the drug epidemic. I was blown away. People who I was close to had become addicted to crack cocaine. They walked the streets like zombies and would wander into our house, and I would direct them out. They talked to themselves and exhibited bizarre behavior. It was a strange sight to see. They had no recollection as to who I was. They would ask me for money and even try to sell me stolen merchandise. Furthermore, some of my friends became big-time drug dealers. They had flashy cars and wore the latest designer clothes. My brother Dino introduced me to the drug game. He sold pure cocaine, never mixing it with baking soda or other substances with the hopes of making more money. I used to watch him cut it with a razor blade and put it in packages to sell for $50.00 a pop. I learned early on how to package drugs. I can't count the number of friends I lost to drug-related crimes. The influx of drugs and guns in the city brought crime to a fever pitch. Gary eventually garnered the reputation of being one of the most dangerous cities in America, and in 1994, became the murder capital of the United States.

Chapter 2

FINDING MY PLACE

My mother came from a large musical family. Everyone either played an instrument, could sing, or was dually gifted. One of the most popular songs I recall us all singing went, "Same train carry my mother… same train carry my father." This song has been in my family for years and was sung at my grandparents' funerals. It still touches me to this day. From time to time my aunts and uncles would get together for jam sessions. They would break out their instruments and it was on! Aunt Barbara would serve as the choir director and the harmony was pitch perfect. They would go on singing and playing for hours as my relatives and I took it all in. It was a family tradition.

My mother used music in a very unique way to motivate my siblings and me. In the wee hours in the morning, I would hear her singing throughout the house. I knew it was only an amount of time before she would start to wake us up to clean the house. Sometimes it would be 2 or 3 o'clock in the morning. As she would do so, she continued to sing as if nothing was wrong. I was tired and agitated. She would always say, "God blessed me with all these children, there's no reason why I shouldn't have a clean house." Afterwards, she would make us go to the living room to have morning devotional. She would read various bible verses and talk to us about what we learned. Then, she would require us to sing. I thought she had lost her mind because we

Principal Michael McGrone Sr.

A few of the McGrone klan

had to go to school in just a few hours! My mother would act as if she were the choir director. I was responsible for bass/tenor notes, my sisters sang soprano, and everyone else sang alto. She was so serious and we all hated it because it was so early in the morning; we just wanted to go back to bed. Over time, we begin to embrace the songs she taught us, which included "Together with Jesus," "Bind Us Together in Love," "Jesus Bless My Mommy," "Get Away, Dog," "Bless This Day Lord" and many more. After all these years, we still get together and sing these songs at family events. It has become part of our family tradition. Though my mother faced mental health challenges, she used her gift of music to keep us together as a family.

One morning, my mother woke us up as usual to clean the house. It was about 3 A.M.; however, we couldn't find my baby brother, Kenyon. We panicked! We searched everywhere looking for him. We thought he ran away. However, my intuition led me to the closet upstairs. I began looking on the shelf and on the floor. I saw a suitcase laying flat on the floor in the corner, so I opened it, and low and behold, there he was. Somehow, Kenyon was able to fit his body in a fetal position inside the suitcase. He was sound asleep. He was determined to get his rest. It was the most hilarious thing I had ever witnessed.

In the early 80's, my parents were given a vintage upright piano. The piano reminded me of those seen in the bar scenes in old Westerns. Rodney and I learned how to play the piano by ear, and we would play for hours until our fingers would cramp. Some of the ivory keys were chipped and would cut into our skin when we played. It didn't bother us because we enjoyed playing and making music. Playing the piano was our escape from reality; it put us in a happy place. Rodney and I won our very first talent show playing together at the Gary Public Library by beating a young lady who actually knew how to properly read music. I was 12 years old and Rodney was 11. I don't play as much as I use to; however, Rodney continues to play and even makes his own music. When we get together, we play the songs from when we were kids and it's like we never missed a beat.

Academically, I never saw school as a place where I could excel. I failed most of my classes and had to catch up. I attended summer school or night school every year. Additionally, I needed eyeglasses, but my parents could not afford them. I would go from K-12 without prescription glasses, which I desperately needed. None of my teachers knew the extent of what I was experiencing at home. All they knew was that I came off as a shy, insecure student who never really put forth much effort. My self-esteem was very low and I never believed in myself. My mother reminded me often that I was one of her most marginal children, at best, and I believed her.

Principal Michael McGrone Sr.

I didn't have many friends my freshman year of high school; all of my friends went to the neighboring Horace Mann High School. However, I wanted to attend Emerson School for the Visual and Performing Arts because of all of the great things I had heard about the school. They had a wide offering of majors, which included dance, piano, art and vocal music. Emerson would give me an opportunity to hone my skills as a piano player. I also wanted to surround myself with other talented individuals. The challenge I faced was that I didn't know how to read music. However, I could play by ear very well. When I auditioned, I did so well that I got accepted. I was excited, but it would be a big mistake in weeks to come. Students who enrolled in Emerson VPA came from all over the city. They were very talented and I felt out of place. Many of them had been there since the school opened and had their established cliques already. I didn't know anyone and felt isolated.

Also, learning to read music would prove to be more difficult than I expected. Reading music was like learning a new language; I did quite poorly. My music teacher suggested that I take piano lessons to catch up with the rest of my classmates because they were so much more advanced than I was, but my parents could not afford for me to take extra lessons. Unable to afford piano lessons, excelling in class became very difficult. Thus, the following year I was allowed to change my major to vocal music. Being in the choir at Emerson, I had quite the experience. Ms. Cowans was the choir director and she was serious about her craft. She was truly a legend. The students in the class were very talented, and could *really* sing. However, I was average at best. I could hold a note, but they were far more talented than I was. The choir was well-known throughout the city. We won numerous awards. Ms. Cowans instilled in us a sense of pride about our history. She wanted us to understand the struggles of African Americans and taught us to become the embodiment of the songs we sung. We would sing in the hall right outside the class; the acoustics were simply amazing. Chills would go through listeners' bodies. The blending sounds of altos, tenors, and the sopranos were breathtaking.

Dino played a major role in exposing me to various soulful artists. We would listen to music for hours. When my parents would leave home, he would put the "hi-fi" outside on the front porch and play Earth, Wind & Fire, Stanley Clarke, Chaka Kahn, Stevie Wonder, the Isley Brothers, Marvin Gaye, Parliament-Funkadelics, and the Doobie Brothers, to name just a few. These were great times. He could also sing, play the drums, and produce his own music. He would have my siblings and I practicing for hours. Somehow, he believed that we would become the next Jackson Five to come out of Gary, but it never came to fruition. He is a perfectionist. He still makes music to this day and is very talented.

One thing that I excelled at was football. I started playing football at the age of eight with the Gary Steelers midget team. All of my friends in the neighborhood played, so I decided to join, too – I wanted to be part of something. I can still remember the first day of practice. I didn't know what to expect. I wore brown corduroy pants and a long sleeve shirt. It was so hot that day. All I could remember was heat and concrete. I was there with all of the other newcomers. Coach laid out his expectations and right there we set out to run a mile around the track of Tolleston's Junior High School. It was hard to run because the track was not paved. It was full of gravel and when we ran it kicked up a lot of dust. The coach's intentions were to weed out players who he thought didn't have the heart to play. As I was running around the track, I was exhausted and hot. In addition, the clothes made it even more uncomfortable. I was not in shape. I was struggling, so the team captain got behind me and began pushing me for encouragement, but I hated it. I started crying, but I was able to finish. Quitting was not an option. I was not about to have my friends make fun of me because I quit. Football gave me an outlet to express my anger in a controlled environment.

Emerson School for the Visual and Performing Arts did not have any sports programs, so I petitioned the school board to play football at the nearby Roosevelt High School. They had great athletes there and I wanted to be apart of a long-standing tradition. It took an entire year to complete the process. Finally, my sophomore year (1987), I was able to play football for

My Sophomore Year at Gary Roosevelt H.S.

Roosevelt High School. I became the first student in the city of Gary to attend one high school, but play sports for another. I was proud to be the first. Soon thereafter, other students at Emerson VPA followed suit and began playing sports at various high schools through the city. Playing football boosted my self-esteem. I did not feel isolated because I was able to excel. My first year at Roosevelt, I was criticized by players on the team because I went to Emerson VPA. Emerson garnered the reputation of having "soft" male students and I was more determined than ever to eradicate that myth. I wanted to play linebacker but I needed to work on my technique, so the head coach, Taliaferro, put me with the linemen. I hated it. They were much bigger and stronger than I was, so being forced to go up against them made me fearless. All the challenges I endured in my first season made me work even harder during the off season. I spent the entire summer working out; I totally transformed my body and would become one of the most feared players on the football team. I became known as a ferocious hitter. When we had tackling drills, players would change places in line to avoid being hit by me. It became personal because of all the taunts I received. I was growing athletically, but by the time I reached my junior year I dislocated my kneecap in a freak accident during practice. As I was completing a tackling drill that I had done hundreds of times before, my kneecap popped out of place. I fell to the ground in excruciating pain, and had to be helped off the field. In the coming days, my knee swelled so badly that it became difficult to walk. I was informed by the doctor that my knee was severely dislocated, and that because I needed to undergo reconstructive knee surgery, I would miss the entire season. I was devastated! I was such a football fanatic that the first thing I asked my mother after surgery was when I would be able to play again. She thought I was nuts, but I was even more determined to return even stronger. I worked hard over the summer. I ran up and down the stadium bleachers until the point of exhaustion. I also worked out several times a week. I knew how to get my body back into top shape. My oldest brother, Dino, taught me everything I needed to know.

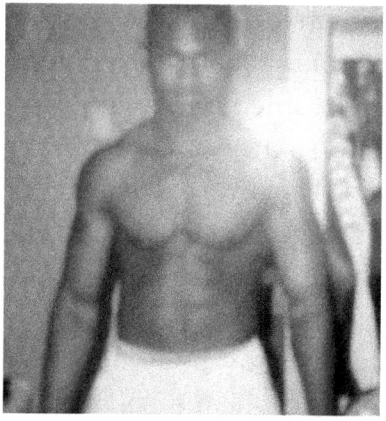

Junior Year Roosevelt H.S.

Chapter 3

❖

DINO

Dino was the prodigal victim of my mother's wrath and dysfunction. He became the outward manifestation of my mother's inner turmoil. My mother was sixteen years old when Dino was born. Despite being diagnosed with severe scoliosis, which often renders natural childbirth an impossibility, her mother, "Mu", refused to allow the doctors to perform a cesarean section . Labor was excruciatingly painful. Nonetheless, after three days of labor, on August 14th, she gave birth to a son. She was not prepared emotionally to take on the responsibility of raising a child, and Dino was subjected to her physical and emotional abuse, as he and my mother essentially grew up together.

It was just my mother and him for eight full years before nine other children were thrust upon him. Many times he had to babysit. He loved my siblings and I; however, he had a hard time showing us his emotions. He took the pain of growing up with a young insecure mother and a rarely-in-the-picture father out on innocent children.

His freshman year in high school, Dino dropped out because he never felt adequate. My mother's lack of self-confidence was perpetuated in his own self-image. Though he was talented, could play the drums, box, and had the looks to model, she never allowed him to pursue the gifts that others saw in him. As a result, he would spend the rest of his life pursuing dreams robbed of him as a young man.

Dino and I were thick as thieves. When I was a baby, he would show me off to his friends. He never allowed them to touch me if their hands weren't clean. I was his first brother and he finally had somebody he could hang out with. Everywhere he went, he would take me along with him. He could walk for miles; I was really small, so every one step he took, it took would take me several steps to catch up with him. He never slowed down, so when he was in a rush, he would put me inside of his coat, zip it up, and start running. I remember him running as fast as he could, breathing heavy as I jostled around inside his coat. I loved it because I wanted to hang out with him and I cried when he would leave without me. It was so much fun! He was my hero. I have many fond memories of our relationship; however, the relationship I had with him would disintegrate over time due to his own demons.

Dino started bodybuilding in his teens and was well-known in Gary for his size. He had 22-inch biceps and could bench press well over 500 pounds. He would use his size to intimidate people. When he walked on the sidewalk, he would make you walk around him. However, on this particular day, a guy refused to move out of his way and they bumped each other. They exchanged words, and the guy went to the trunk of his car to retrieve a shotgun. He started walking toward us. I was scared to death! Dino told me to run, so I took off as fast as I could. I didn't run too far because I was concerned about what might happen to my brother, so I hid in some bushes that were nearby. I wanted to be close to help him if anything happened. Somehow, he was able to finagle his way out of it. I didn't care what he did, as long as he came back in one piece.

Unfortunately, this would not be the last time. Dino had a knack

Me at 15 and Rodney 14

for making people angry. I recall one incident when he threatened all of the young men on the block where we lived. They were furious and wanted to immediately fight him. They found Dino at a currency exchange on Broadway and demanded that he come outside. He explained that he had no problem fighting, but that he wanted to do so one-on-one. However, they relented because Dino was known for having superior boxing skills. Though he may have said he wanted to fight one-on-one, I knew he could handle several of them at one time. I had also seen him knock people out with only one punch. He had a tough reputation and he wore it like a badge of honor.

Dino won numerous bodybuilding competitions and awards. He also trained people who would eventually become well-known bodybuilders in Gary. He started training my brother Rodney and I when we turned fourteen. He kept a bucket next to the bench press and when I asked him what it was going to be used for, he said it was there for when I threw up. I thought he was joking, but he was right. His workouts were so intense I vomited quite often. He had a way of getting into your head to make you believe you were invincible. He always reminded me when I threw up that it was simply pain leaving the body. He called me the "Machine" and I believed him. I worked out to muscle failure. I literally couldn't pick my arms up to wipe the sweat off my forehead. After workouts, we would run through the neighborhood. Each corner we arrived at, he made us get down to do push-ups on his count. We were a lot bigger and stronger than most boys our age and we gained a lot of respect. Dino also taught us how to fight and would always tell us that a fight was never fair, that anything goes. He made us put our hands behind our back as he punched us in the stomach and if you started to cry, he got angry. After a while, we learned how to withstand his powerful blows. He was preparing us for the tough streets of Gary. We became his protégés. He taught me never to show signs of weakness, even if I felt physical or emotional pain. This would be detrimental to me in the years to come, because I never showed anyone my true feelings. I became good at internalizing

Rodney And I working at Bally's Health Club

how I truly felt. Dino wanted me to be tough and if I showed him any signs of vulnerability he would tell me to, "Suck that up." He said the streets were no place for punks and made sure I was in fighting trim. He was intense.

We had a punching bag that weighed well over 200 pounds. The bag was slightly worn, and we punched it until our shoulders would start to burn. The skin would also peel off my knuckles and I would bleed because I didn't wear gloves. I didn't complain because I wanted Dino to know that I could handle the pain. This was our warm-up exercise before we started weight training. Because we trained religiously, Rodney and I transformed our bodies. We were competitive with each other. We would walk around our neighborhood, showing off our chiseled torsos. We both won the best physique award our junior and senior years in high school. Rodney would go on to compete professionally and win numerous body building competitions.

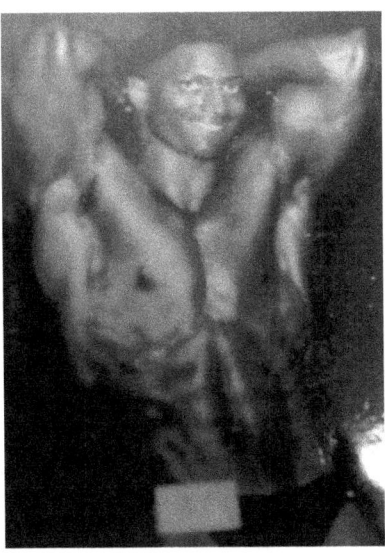

Rodney in a body building competition in his early 20's

Principal Michael McGrone Sr.

At the height of the drug epidemic in Gary, Dino bought an infield 45 semi-automatic handgun. It was huge and had a cartridge that could hold fifteen bullets at one time. He had this fascination with guns. He would buy gun magazines and tell me which gun he wanted to purchase. He loved the power and the damage they could inflict on a body. He loved showing his guns off, too. Many times he would carry them around in broad daylight. It was like the Wild West. The infield .45 had a hairline trigger. I remember him almost shooting himself in the foot as he carried the gun by his side. The blast was so powerful that it pierced through the concrete. It scared the heck out of him and me.

The scariest moment occurred when he was in his apartment. His girlfriend and I were with him as he sat on the bed. He jokingly put the gun to his head. His girlfriend ordered him to stop. She asked, "What if you accidentally shoot yourself?"

He told her that he had removed the cartridge from the gun and that she didn't have anything to worry about. This really made both of us nervous. She told him that to be on the safe side, to first shoot the gun toward the ceiling before pulling the trigger on himself. When he did, the gun went off, blowing a hole in the ceiling. I remember it being so loud and intense. He could have blown his brains out right in front of us. When he removed the clip, he forgot to clear the chamber and the results could have been deadly. I was traumatized! I definitely learned about gun safety that day. Dino taught me how to shoot, remove the cartridge, and empty the chamber. The first gun I shot was a 22 caliber pistol when I was about twelve years old. It was broad daylight and I fired outside the kitchen window. The kick was strong and it made me feel powerful.

It was not unusual to hear gunshots throughout the day and

night in our neighborhood. When we heard shots, we would get on our knees and peer through the curtains to see if we could tell where they were coming from. When the firing ceased, we simply continued on with our day as if nothing had happened. In hindsight it was crazy, but that was our normal. The police were hardly ever called because it happened so frequently.

Dino exposed me to quite a bit at a young age. His addiction to pornography would have a profound impact on my perception of women. He bought numerous sex tapes and magazines. When he would have sex, he would hide my brothers and me in the closet to watch him perform. His goal was to educate us about sex. Though his intentions were good, it distorted my idea of a healthy relationship. Additionally, he would put me on the phone with his girlfriends and make me call them derogatory names. I hated it because it made me feel extremely uncomfortable. I wanted it to stop; however, I didn't want him to disapprove of me. To this day, I have never referred to a woman using any disrespectful words. It brings back negative memories of the conversations I had with his girlfriends. I also hated when my friends used such words to describe women. I became even more extreme, breaking off relationships I had with women who used explicit language.

Furthermore, he exposed me to gay and transgender men. While he never professed to being gay, even though I was fairly young, I knew something was different. I struggled with the contradiction of him being "straight," but constantly hanging around gay and transgender men. One night, he took me with him to this place that was full of transgender men. It was dark, gloomy, and smoky. This place scared the crap out of me and I wanted to leave immediately. There were men dressed up in wigs, high heels and mini-skirts. They looked strange; I felt so uncomfortable. I had never seen anything like that before. To this day, I never questioned my brother as to why he took me there; I was just relieved that we left.

My most traumatic, life-altering experience came in the summer of 1988. My siblings and I were home alone; my mother spent a night at the hospital tending to my father who was recovering from a stroke. As I was watching T.V. in the family room, I heard the front door open, and then a big commotion. Jamie came into the family room crying. I asked what happened. He told me that Dino slapped him and I was furious! I was tired of all the years of abuse our brother put my siblings and me through. I expressed my disgust with Jamie as to what took place and to my surprise, Dino overheard what I said. He came storming into the room, and got in my face.

"Boy, you tough now, huh? Okay, we gon' see how tough you really are."

I went into the kitchen, along with Rodney and Jamie. Dino returned to the house with a sawed-off shotgun. I was standing in front of the stove and he commanded, "Boy, say 'I'm sorry,'" but I refused.

He said it again, "Boy, I will blow yo' head off……say I'm sorry."

He rested the gun on my chest as his finger was on the trigger. Jamie and Rodney started crying, pleading with me to say I was sorry, but I refused. That night I had reached my breaking point, and I was not afraid of him anymore. My refusal upset him even more, so he put the gun point-blank to my head and cocked the trigger back. He reiterated, "I'm going to tell you one last time to say you're sorry," but I still didn't. Within a flash, the gun went off. My ears were ringing and everything went silent. I couldn't hear a thing, due to the shotgun blast being so close to my head. I could taste gunpowder in my mouth.

The whole thing happened so fast. Glass and wood chips flew everywhere because the blast just missed my head by inches, blowing the kitchen window out. At this point, I was petrified. My heart was racing a hundred miles per hour and I took off outside. Everything slowed down as if it was happening in slow motion. I ran around the block and eventually stood between the houses directly across the street from our house. I could see Dino reclining on the porch with the gun between his legs. He screamed out, "Boy, I'm waiting for you!"

Eventually, I returned to the house after being outside for hours. I was too exhausted to care what happened at that point. I entered the house and he told me to patch up the hole from the gunshot blast; I told him I wasn't doing anything. He then fixed it himself using Scotch tape and brown shoe polish. I met with my siblings and told them not to tell Momma anything. We never called the police either.

My mother returned home the following morning and we all welcomed her as if nothing happened. We were more concerned about how she was feeling, knowing that my father was in grave condition. My thoughts were not to burden her because she had enough to worry about. She wouldn't find out what happened until years later. My father went to his grave never knowing what happened. My father could no longer protect us, so I took it upon myself to protect my family. After years of abuse, I was finally no longer afraid of Dino. I was willing to do whatever it took to protect my family, even if it meant losing my life. I carried the pain of my brother putting a gun to my head for decades. I was hurt because we were so close. He practically raised me, and

The hole from the shot gun blast 25 years later

I never thought he would do something like that to me. For years, I didn't have anyone to talk to; I had nowhere to turn. I recall going to school the next day, very disillusioned. I couldn't focus. I would have nightmares of being killed or of me killing someone. The dreams would awaken me in the middle of the night and I would sweat profusely. It all seemed so real that I would cry myself back to sleep. I never confided the pain I was feeling to anyone; I suffered in silence. I didn't know that I was suffering from post-traumatic stress disorder (PTSD) until much later in life. I went back to visit my childhood home in 2013 and remnants of the gunshot blast were still there. You could still see where someone had tried to fill in the hole where the gunshot blast pierced through the side of the window. All of the memories came rushing back and I became very emotional. In that same year (2013), I decided to take a trip to visit Dino. The sole purpose of me taking this trip was to forgive myself and for Dino to move on with his life. For some reason, I knew he anguished over the incident for years. I wanted closure for both of us. Because our relationship had been estranged, I hadn't seen him in over ten years. Upon arriving to his house, I called to let him know that I was out front. He came out to greet me. I was nervous. I could tell that he was nervous, as well. My friend took pictures of the whole encounter. We embraced each other, which seemed to go on for hours. We cried in each other arms over all the years we had lost. We were different people now. He kept saying, "I'm sorry, Mike... I'm sorry, Mike."

I hugged him even tighter. I knew he was referring to the gun incident. He pulled away, gazing at me with tears in his eyes and said, "I guess you not lil Mike anymore?"

Dino and me meeting for the first time in 10 years

He told me he couldn't believe that I turned out to be the person I am today. I told him that I was no longer carrying the guilt and the pain of what he had done. I wanted him to sleep at night knowing that I was at peace. I knew that his health was declining and I didn't want anything to happen to him without him knowing that I had forgiven him; I wanted to bury that part of our lives for good. I felt a sense of relief after our reunion. Following this encounter, we would catch up on all the years we had lost.

There were several contradictions in our relationship. I knew that he loved me; however, he had a difficult time showing it. In fact, he loved all of our siblings; he just had a hard time showing it, being a victim of abuse himself.

He believed in education (though he never graduated from high school) and would always encourage me to do my best. I had perfect attendance during my K-12 years. He always explained how education would be my ticket out of the ghetto. Though I didn't perform well in school, it would be his inspirational talks that would motivate me when I would experience my greatest challenge during my first year in college. He taught me that the world owes you nothing and that you have to work hard for what you want. I would carry that trait with me for the rest of my life. Dino was fearless and intense about everything. My success in overseeing school programs is directly related to the values he instilled in me. He made me the fearless leader I am today. This incident with Dino putting the gun to my head would have devastating implications in years to come (I'll explain in Chapter 6). Dino lives a quiet life in Texas. He has evolved as a human being. I hope that his latter years are his best. I want him to know that through it all I still love him. Despite the complexities of our relationship, I will never forget his part in molding me into the man I am today.

Chapter 4

THE DEATH OF SUPERMAN

My father in his early 20's

In the spring of 1988, I returned home after serving a half-day of school. Uncle Preston was unexpectedly at the house. My mother told us that something went terribly wrong with my father, so we ran upstairs. While lying in bed, we noticed that his face was contorted and that he did not have control of the right side of his body. We quickly hoisted him up, placed his arm around our shoulders, and immediately took him to the hospital. We rushed him to the hospital as quickly as we could.

Upon arriving there, the doctors discovered that my father had experienced a massive stroke. When they placed him on the gurney, I remember him crying, saying to me that he couldn't do it anymore (i.e., work, supporting the family, protecting us). That was the first time I saw my father cry, and it made me emotional. He said that he needed me to step up. At that moment, I knew that my life would never be the same. In the days ahead, my father's health began to decline, so they transferred him to another hospital and placed him in the Intensive Care Unit (ICU) where they could provide around-the-clock care. My siblings and I took shifts spending the night at his bedside. He had tubes coming from everywhere, including a feeding tube connected to his stomach. He couldn't talk because of the equipment and pain, and he only spoke to us through his eyes.

Within a few months, my father's health would start to improve and the doctors allowed him to return home for the holidays. However, he was still restricted to the gurney. Everything that was in his hospital room was in his room at our house. My father was weak and couldn't walk, so I would lift him out of bed and place him in his wheelchair. He wanted to see more of the house, but the house was not wheelchair-accessible. My father would repeatedly say to me, "Michael, pick me up, pick me up!" so I would literally pick him up from his wheelchair and walk with him throughout the house. He would say, "My son... my son, you've gotten so strong." Though my father lost a lot of weight, he was still fairly large. I felt both sad and proud that I could pick my father up because he had carried me for so long.

Wednesday, December 14, 1988, seemed to be a normal night as usual. My mother had just finished feeding my father through the feeding tube and bathing him. He called me to the room at about 10:30 P.M. I had to lift him up because he was too weak to do it on his own; his shoulder rested on mine as I sat next to him. The conversation I had with him was like nothing I ever had before. He fixed his eyes on mine as he told me to promise him that I would never drink or get high. He also wanted me to promise him that I would attend college and finish. I had great respect for my father and was determined to make good on these promises. He sacrificed so much to make my life better. I asked him, "You're gonna be with me though, right?"

He replied, "Son, I can't do it anymore."

Somehow, he knew that death was near and he was preparing me for what would inevitably become my reality. At about 11:15 P.M., my mother summoned my siblings and I into my father's room, with panic in her voice. We all stood shocked alongside his bed as he was struggling to breathe; you could see his eyes dilating. He was fighting for his life. My mother started praying. I was pleading with my father not to leave us like this. It was emotionally overwhelming. Everything was happening so fast. By this time, the ambulance arrived. One of the ambulance attendants was a member of the church we attended. We knew he was in good hands. When they hoisted him out of bed, my father's body went limp. They rushed him out of the house into the back of the ambulance. I followed right behind them.

It was a cold and snowy night. With my face pressed firmly against the window of the ambulance, the medics went right to work on him. They used the defibrillator to revive him. They also took turns doing CPR. Soon thereafter they sped off, and I ran as fast as I could to the hospital (which was only 15 minutes away). When I arrived in the waiting area, Dino, Kim and Michelle were already there. Within 10 minutes, the doctor came into the waiting room to talk to us. He started asking us questions and making comments about my father like, "What kind of work did your father do?" and "Your father was a big man."

I was initially relieved. He gave us the impression that everything was okay and that my father survived, so I asked how he was doing. Then, to my surprise, the doctor said, "I'm sorry, Mr. McGrone didn't make it."

I asked, "What do you mean, Mr. McGrone didn't make it?"

He repeated the dreaded words. "I'm sorry, Mr. McGrone didn't make it." It was surreal. It was like I was having an out-of-body experience. I didn't believe him, so I ran into the recovery room where my father's body lay lifeless. I began screaming at him.

"Don't leave me like this, I can't do this by myself!"

I started shaking the gurney because he wouldn't respond to me; however, he was already gone. My father was dead. Security was called and I had to be escorted out of the hospital. I ran back home in the snowy conditions as fast as I could in an emotional rage. I was too numb to feel anything. I was crying and disillusioned. When I arrived home, my mother met me at the front door. She knew by the look on my face that he was gone. I went into his room and tore it apart. I was angry and my mother didn't do anything to stop me. Tired and drained from all of the crying, I fell asleep on the living room floor. The whole ordeal felt like a bad dream. However, when I woke up the next morning, reality set in. I saw my aunts, uncles, family and friends arrive at the house to offer their condolences. It was not a dream; my father was really gone. My eyes were nearly swollen shut from all the crying. My father's death would change the trajectory of my life.

On the day of my father's funeral, it all felt unreal. The world seemed entirely different. I grew up, and everyone would soon know I was taking over the throne my father entrusted me with. My classmates from Emerson VPA attended the funeral, and it felt good to have their love and support. Everyone spoke about the impacts my father made in their lives. I closed out the speeches, letting everyone know about his legacy and what he meant to our family. As we left the funeral, I saw siblings from my father's first wife who I haven't seen in years. It would be the first time that most of us were gathered together in one place. When we returned from the funeral, family and friends met at our house for the repast. The house was packed. It was a somber occasion, as expected. Everyone was eating while others were crying and hugging each other. All of a sudden, we heard gunfire coming from the side of the house. My uncles rushed outside to see what was going on and saw Dino firing a sawed-off shotgun. They had to subdue him. It was his way of expressing anger toward family members he thought never really cared about my father. It was also his way of venting about the loss of the man who truly showed him love.

Things got really bad after my father died. We rarely had enough food to eat and we never seemed to be able to keep the utility bills afloat. When the city would disconnect our water, our neighbor June knew how to turn it back on. He also knew how to restore our electricity when it was disconnected. When the electric company got wind of what we were doing, they removed the entire electrical unit from the house. Every time they would cut off the utilities, my mother would create a new account by putting the utility bill in one of the kids' names to circumvent paying the bill. However, after doing this a few times, the utility company refused to allow anyone who resided in the home with the last name McGrone to get the utilities put back on. As funny as it may sound, our credit was bad even as children.

To make ends meet, I got a job working as a stock boy at Tim's Broadway Pharmacy. I would steal detergent, food, and other household items to help out at home. I would have my mother pull up to the back of the store and I would put groceries in the car as she drove off as quickly as she could.

Soon after my father's death, my mother filed to receive Social Security benefits in my name, and because I was 18, I always refused to hand it over to her. This caused major battles, however, I felt that I could do a better job managing my portion. Our monthly mortgage bill was no more than a few hundred dollars a month. Despite having food stamps, a substantial insurance payout from my father's death, and a large social security payment each month, we still struggled to keep the utilities on and food in the house. It didn't resonate with me as much then, but now I wonder what my mother did with all of that money. I can remember her buying furniture for the house and other household items, but nothing added up to the amount of money she received each month. It was a constant struggle. After the death of my father, we tried to develop a new norm. However, the atmosphere became extremely morbid, and everyone tried to cope with the absence of my father as best they could. My siblings and I were constantly hurting and felt helpless. With the passing of my father, I became the man of the house, and I wore it like a badge of honor. I was following in my father's footsteps.

I was a sub-par student, but after the death of my father my grades plummeted even further. I was a zombie. I would wake up, go to school, and zone out through an entire day's worth of instruction. School became irrelevant. I was going through the motions, using my motor skills with no emotional charge. Things would get much worse before they got better.

In the year 2000, in just a little over a decade, we lost our home to foreclosure, despite government assistance. This would mark the end of the life we knew at 413 Madison Street. We lost the home that "Superman" worked so hard to keep. I did everything I could, including taking out loans to pay the mortgage, but the burden became too great. I could no longer afford to both pay for college and pay the mortgage. I was devastated and felt that I had failed everyone, especially my father.

Chapter 5

COLLEGE MATERIAL

On the day I graduated from high school, we did not have electricity or gas. The utilities had been shut off for the past several months. I had to use a flashlight to find my clothes for graduation, and I was furious. I told my mother I didn't want anybody coming to my graduation, so my mother dropped me off at Wirt High School where the graduation ceremony was taking place. All of my classmates were elated during the festivities and were giving each other congratulatory hugs, posing for pictures, and laughing. I was isolated and withdrawn; however, I was able to shield the pain by taking pictures with

Jamie and Rodney at my graduation   *Receiving my high School diploma*

a few of my classmates. Once we were preparing to receive our diplomas, I became anxious. I knew no one would be there to cheer for me when my name was called. However, to my surprise, I heard a loud cheer when my turn was announced; it was my family clapping and cheering me on. My mother had gone against my wishes and attended anyway. She brought Jamie and Rodney with her. I was happy they came, despite me telling them not to. After the graduation, I went out with my friends and we had a great time. We celebrated the night away. When they brought me home, it was embarrassing because not one light was on in the house and some of my siblings were sitting outside on the front porch. It looked odd. I was glad they didn't question me about it.

I was confused about what I wanted to do after high school. I graduated at the bottom of my class with a 1.2 GPA, and I didn't apply to any colleges because I didn't think I was college material. I took the ASVAB test to enlist in the Army, but my scores were too low. I felt terrible. I was not even smart enough to fight in the Army! On a fluke, I end up going to Southeastern Academy in Kissimmee, Florida because a friend of mine was going. He said that it was a good school and that you did not have to take an entrance exam, nor did they consider your GPA for admission. I thought it was the perfect fit. Southeastern Academy trained students in the hospitality field, and boasted that jobs would be plentiful once we completed the program.

The day I left for Southeastern Academy was emotional for my family and me. I had been the father figure of the clan and I was leaving them for the first time. As I boarded the Greyhound bus to be transported to the airport, all of my siblings were standing alongside the bus, crying. I was an emotional wreck, but I felt that I needed to make something of my life. I was 19 years old and had never been on a plane before, so the entire experience was an adventure.

When I arrived in Kissimmee, Florida, it was really pretty. I saw palm trees for the first time and the weather was very nice. The buildings and homes were colorful and people dressed differently to adjust to the warm climate. There was also a strong presence from ethnic groups from all over the world. It was a culture shock to me. When I introduced myself to my peers and told them where I was from, they were reluctant to get to know me. They had heard all of the horror stories about Gary and thought I was a bad person who sought out trouble. However, I quickly changed that perception. I gained quite a few friends and we had a ball. I was not the shy Michael anymore. We traveled to Daytona Beach and other popular attractions in Florida to party.

The classes were really easy and the teachers were hands-on. I finished the program within several months and got a certificate of completion. As odd as it may seem, I wanted to be a Flight Attendant.

When I returned to Gary, I thought I was well-prepared for my new career path. However, after applying for numerous jobs, I was continuously rejected. I felt frustrated and depressed. No one in our home was employed; we were all just *existing*. I felt my motivation deteriorating and was tired and desperate. I hit rock-bottom and was willing to do whatever I had to change my reality. My Uncle Abraham was a well-known radio personality in Gary. He knew professional athletes and had a relationship with Pat McCaskey, a Chicago Bears board member. After Abraham explained my situation to him, Mr. McCaskey recommended that I attend Triton College in River Grove, IL. They had programs that could help me academically and also develop my skills as an outside linebacker.

Uncle Abraham took me on several visits, and I fell in love with the school. It was the first time I had been on a college campus, and I was immediately captivated. I had an opportunity to talk to Coach Mitz, the head football coach. He spoke about the academic support I would receive and how if I worked hard I could earn a starting position as a linebacker. I was excited to get started. As I prepared for college, my cousin Darryl bought me my first pair of eyeglasses in August of 1990. I went to an optometrist for the

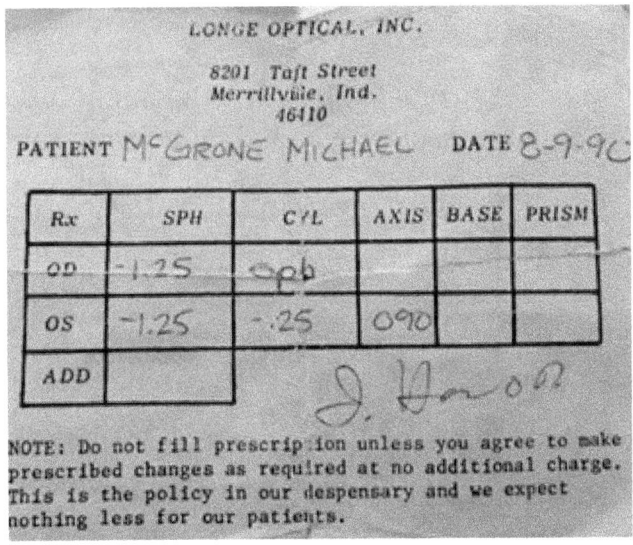

My prescription to receive glasses.

first time in my life. I had needed glasses since childhood, but my parents couldn't afford them. I saw the world and my goals clearly for the first time. Life was becoming clearer, both literally and figuratively. I kept the prescription after all of these years, thankful for Darryl's generosity. I always had great respect for

Principal Michael McGrone Sr.

Cousin Vincent and my mother

him because he was consistently there for me after my father died, and he gave me good advice and became my role model.

I left home with only a blue suitcase (one of the latches was broken) and the clothes on my back. I had several pairs of underwear, two pairs of pants, three shirts, and a few pictures of my family. I also had $50 in my pocket. As I said my good-byes, my mother yelled out, "Oh, you'll be back... You know you're not college material!"

She always reminded me that I was not the brightest of her children. Nevertheless, I was extremely focused. Nothing was going to deter me. My cousin Vincent waited for me outside to take me to school. We left in a silver-colored (spray-painted), two-door Escort. It was the ugliest car you could imagine, and it was a stick shift. It could only seat two. Nevertheless, I was grateful he took the time out of his schedule to take me to school. When we arrived at Triton College, the car broke down. We barely made it (the car broke down once we made it to campus). He dropped me off near the football stadium. He never asked me

Triton College Football Team photo (I'm in the center, #58)

where I would be staying and neither did I think about it at the time. I walked into the sports center to let Coach Mitz know that I had arrived. I got my football gear and hung out in the locker room until practice started. I met guys from all over the country, and everyone was really cool. We ran and went through a series of football agility exercises.

Once practice was over, I started to get nervous because everyone was preparing to go home, and I didn't have anywhere to go. I pulled Coach Mitz to the side and told him about my situation and he was floored! He asked why I would apply to college without having first established residency. I told him I didn't have the money and that I was waiting on my financial aid check to arrive. He brought the entire football team back on the field and gathered everyone in a circle and asked if anyone had any extra room for me to stay at their place temporarily. A teammate by the name of Jean volunteered to allow me to stay with him at his parents' house in Evanston. I tried to be invisible because I knew I was a stranger in their house and didn't have anywhere else to go. They provided me with a cover and I slept on the couch. They also fed me. I didn't have any money to contribute and knew it was only a matter of time before I would be asked to leave. After a couple of weeks, that became the case. Jean felt bad telling me that I had to pick up my things and leave, but I truly understood. I had become a burden to the family. I was grateful that I had a place to lay my head for a while. I would end up moving in with various guys on the football team several more times.

In a garden apartment in Maywood, I stayed with five of my teammates in a one-bedroom apartment. Space was tight. My two teammates whose names were on the lease got the room, Simpson slept in the food pantry; Torren and I slept in the living room. We spent many nights talking about life and what we wanted to achieve. I didn't have a mattress, cover, or pillow, so I slept on top of towels to cushion my body from the hard floor. I always slept with my clothes on to stay warm and to keep the roaches from crawling on me. Sometimes it would get so cold at night that I would wait for Torren to fall into a deep sleep and snatch the covers off him. If that didn't work, I would sleep close enough that I could wrap myself in the cover hanging off his bed. Sometimes I would sleep in the bath tub to stay warm and safe from the roaches. Times were tough, and I was willing to do whatever I had, to avoid returning to Gary. I was used to living in harsh conditions. Sleeping on the floor was not unusual for me because I had done it at home.

One of the funniest things was seeing Simpson set up the food pantry as if it were a real room; he had posters and all sorts of decorations adorning the walls. We had our food on the shelves and would often disturb him when he was asleep to get food for breakfast, lunch and dinner. He would invite girls over and though he had a curtain rigged for privacy, you could see their feet hanging outside the pantry. It was hilarious!

Food was scarce. We all had our own personal stash. On this particular day, I was starving. We had a tough day of practice. We worked our butts off and I couldn't wait to get home to enjoy a box of fish sticks and French fries. However, when I returned to the apartment, there were only 4 fish sticks left in a box that originally had 40. I was livid! Simpson did not go to practice, so it was obvious that he was the only one that could have eaten my fish sticks. The apartment also reeked of marijuana. When I questioned him about eating my fish sticks, he got defensive.

"Naw man, I ain't eat yo fish sticks. Now get out my face!"

When I questioned him a second time, he walked toward me in an aggressive manner and that's when I punched him in the jaw. Dino had taught me to never let an individual run up on you without defending yourself. We began to tussle. I was punching him relentlessly. Somehow we ended up in the closet. He got a hammer and tried to hit me with it, but somehow I was able to finagle it out of his clenched fist. I then turned the hammer on him. As I tried to strike him, I severely cut my right knee with the hooks on the hammer. On the second attempt, my buddy Walter rushed over and wrestled the hammer out my hand. Had it not been for him I probably would have killed or seriously injured Simpson in an act of rage. My roommates pulled us apart. My adrenaline was still high, so I ran outside with just my pants on and called my mother from a pay phone to tell her what happened. It was cold outside, but I didn't feel a thing. She calmed me down and said she would do her best to help with groceries. My friends didn't know how much I was struggling. They had their parents that they could depend on and I knew my mother was not really in a position to help me. Times were tough and I didn't know where I was going to get my next meal.

The following day we had a football game, and I didn't want Coach Mitz to find out that two of his athletes got into an altercation over food. However, that would prove to be more difficult than I thought. I had a big gash in my right knee and there was no way I could play with an open wound that severe. The trainers did a good job wrapping it up so that I could play. They started questioning me about what happened. I gave them this lame excuse about how I slipped and fell, but word spread quickly as to what really happened. After the game, Coach met with the entire team and discussed the victory and the follow-up practice schedule. I was relieved; somehow I thought he didn't find out what happened. He then talked about his disappointment about teammates getting into a physical altercation over food. He said that no players on his team should ever be fighting over food. The entire ordeal was embarrassing. To this day, my friends still tease me about the incident. They joke, "Don't mess with Mike's fish sticks, he's the only guy we know who will mess you up for eating his fish sticks!" It's funny now, but it wasn't so funny back then.

When my mother came to visit me in the apartment, she started crying. She couldn't believe how I was living. She noticed that I didn't have a bed, cover, or pillow and that I slept on the floor. The apartment also reeked of marijuana and there were people loitering outside. I never considered my living conditions because I was so focused on making something of myself. I didn't have a plan B. She brought me a box full of canned food, and clothes to wear that she got from the local Goodwill. I was so happy to have food that would last me for a couple of weeks. The clothes were old and outdated. I came up with a plan to sell them to anybody who was interested and I made $40; I saved it to buy groceries. Before my mother left to go back home, I reassured her that I would be okay and that in the coming weeks I would be moving into my own apartment; however, that was the farthest thing from the truth. The fact of the matter was, I didn't know where I was going to live. I was at the mercy of whoever I was living with. When they got tired of me, I had to leave.

As things got tense and tight in Maywood, I would find temporary housing through a Triton College employee by the name of Mike. He was the Director of Financial Aid and would later become my mentor and friend. Over time we would develop a trusting relationship. I would even become the godfather for his son, Marcus. Mike was a sharp dresser and drove fancy cars, which was appealing to me. He was articulate and smart. I told him about my housing dilemma and he allowed me to stay at his apartment, rent-free. It would be the first time I had a bed to sleep on since arriving at Triton College. I was grateful for his generosity. I would only stay there for a couple weeks because he was not renewing his lease.

Shortly thereafter, I found a place to live in Oak Park. The house looked beautiful from the outside, but once you entered the house it was a complete dump. The lady who owned the house was a hoarder. I literally had to step over trash to move around in the house. She had a room that she was renting out and I had a few bucks left over from the money I received from financial aid to find temporary shelter. I shared the upstairs with a middle-aged white woman, which made me extremely uncomfortable. Her room was right across the hall from mine. The whole situation was creepy.

The bathroom was located in the hall. On occasions, I would pass her during the night as she was coming out of the bathroom. She didn't utter a word and I was scared to death. I made sure my door stayed locked. I rarely slept, due to all of the strange noises in the house. I wanted to be prepared in the event that someone tried to enter my room. I didn't have any bed linen, so the owner gave me what appeared to be blood-stained sheets. I was grossed out of my mind. There was no way I was going to sleep with those sheets. Within a few weeks I couldn't take it anymore and planned my escape... yes, *escape*! My buddy Mike pulled up to the front of the house and we started throwing my belongings in his car. To our surprise, the owner pulled up directly behind us. Luckily, we finished loading the car up with all my belongings and took off as fast as we could. The whole situation felt like a scene out of a scary movie. She was cursing and yelling. I was glad I was not going to spend another night in that horrid place.

Mr. and Mrs. Dick Andre

The next day at practice, I spoke to Chad, the starting quarterback for Triton College, about my living situation. He told me he had two other roommates, and that they had an extra room available. I told him that I was in a desperate situation and needed a place to stay. He scheduled a meeting for me to meet Dick, who was the homeowner. I told Dick that I didn't have any money to cover rent at the time, but that I would pay him once I received the money from the loans I applied for. I wanted him to trust that I would be a man of my word. He didn't know that this was the end of the rope for me. The only other option for me was sleeping on the streets. I literally didn't know where I was going to lay my head that night. He spoke to me with love and compassion. I felt that he truly cared about me. To my surprise, he said that I could move in. I was overwhelmed. I finally had a place I could call my home. I cried tears of joy. He said that as part of the agreement, I had to promise him that I would graduate from Triton College. I told him that we had a deal.

Honestly, I never knew when the financial aid check would come, so I did whatever I could to make the money I needed for rent. My football teammate, Walter, was a well-known exotic dancer in Chicago. He introduced me to "Tee", and "Klimax" another well-known dancer. These were the sharpest brothers I had ever met. They were well groomed, dressed well and kept fine cars. They were intimidating to the "Average" guy. One infamous night, they gave me a crash course in exotic dancing after Walter begged me to do a show with him at a club called, "Brothers Palace". His friend canceled at the last minute. Until that point, I never would have imagined I was taking my clothes off for money, but I was in a desperate situation and needed the money, so I agreed. Walter insisted I dress in an outfit with green sequins and 'shingles' that hung off the pants and sleeves. I looked like a cowboy. We greased our bodies with baby oil. He told me I would have to take off my prescription strength glasses before the start of the show which meant I couldn't see a thing. We did pushups to get pumped up. Minutes later, the song 'There's Some Whores in This House" began to play and that was our queue to start the show. The song was incredibly disrespectful but I didn't realize it at the time. The important thing to me was making money to pay my rent. My heart was racing. The place was packed with a bunch of screaming ladies. Walter told me to mimic his dance moves and the women started hollering and going crazy when

Walter began gyrating his body; I followed right behind him. They were smacking our butts and pulling wherever they could. Although I didn't know what the heck I was doing, we even gave individual dances. The women were 'making it rain' with money. For all our efforts, we were lavished with loose bills in almost every denomination. After about 20 minutes placating the women, Walter started to remove his clothes and gestured my way, signaling me to do the same. I took off my shirt, but that was as far as I was willing to go. We literally got into an argument on the stage when I refused to take off my pants. The women were screaming in unison for me to "take it off". Still, I refused and danced right off the stage. I just couldn't bear it all. Luckily, that night I was able to make enough money to pay my rent. It was truly one of the most embarrassing moments of my life. That would be the first and final time I would ever strip. Walter's stripping days are long past. He is now happily married with a beautiful family. Walter still jokes about me leaving him on the stage. My response: as far as the audience knew, it was part of the show.

Walter in his early 20's after a show at Sarah J's in Chicago. Walter with his wife and twin girls

Dick became a father figure to me. We spent a lot of time talking about life and all of its complexities. I became part of his family, and many times they invited me over to have dinner with them. Gary's demographics consisted of predominately African American individuals and I was not accustomed to being around white people. My interactions with white people in Gary had mostly been with police officers, which were typically negative situations and therefore I didn't trust them. However, Dick changed that perspective for me and I slowly began to open up to him. He was a good Christian man.

Because of his act of kindness, I was able to graduate from Triton College. I did whatever it took to pass, including taking remedial classes for an entire year and attending tutoring lessons every day after school. It took me three years to finish a two-year Associate of Arts degree, but I persevered. When I got my diploma, I rushed to Dick's house to let him know I made good on my promise. Though it's been well over 25 years, I still call him every year to thank him for his generosity and his unselfishness. He believed in me and gave me a chance. He saved my life and propelled me to where I am today.

At Dick's house the day I graduated from Triton

In the summer of 1992, I worked hard to recover from total knee surgery and received numerous offers to play Division 1 football across the Midwest. However, I chose to attend Northern Illinois University (NIU) because it was only an hour a half from home and I did not want to be far from my family.

My sophomore year at Triton

They knew I had undergone two reconstructive knee surgeries and before granting me a scholarship they wanted to make sure my knee could hold up. My first surgery was my junior year in high school. On a freak accident in practice, I twisted my kneecap out of place, hitting a running back coming out of backfield. I also had torn cartilage. I had run this drill a thousand times before without any problems.

The second incident happened my second year at Triton, where I was hit by a receiver below the waist. The receiver cracked down on my blind side, removing me from the play. While doing so, he hit me with the butt of his helmet directly on the lateral part of my right knee. Instantly, I knew something was wrong. I felt a pop and I fell to the ground in excruciating pain, holding my knee. I couldn't believe it was the same knee I had injured in high school. My teammates gathered around me, demanding that I get up. They didn't know how badly I was hurt. The culture of football is that you never want to show the opposing team that you are hurt. So, I mustered up enough courage and walked off the field with the assistance of my teammates. Staggering back to the bench to receive treatment, I knew my season was over. My knee felt like Jell-O. I couldn't put any weight on it; it had swollen to the size of a watermelon. I had to have surgery to repair it, and it would never be the same again.

During practice at NIU, I never felt like I was 100%. I tried to fake it as much as I could; however, the coaches knew something was wrong. They said I was running with a limp and was afraid I would get hurt. I pleaded my case, saying that I was just tired and exhausted. However, they played a video of me in practice, and you could clearly see that I was hurting. They told me to turn in my equipment. I was devastated! At 23 years old, my football career was over. I had played until my body couldn't take it anymore. I went into the locker room and cried like a baby. As you could imagine, my time at NIU was short-lived.

Chapter 6

❖

A Dream Deferred

In 1993, I packed my bags and left Northern Illinois University. I called Dick and asked him if I could move back into the house. He agreed and said that he would let me stay rent-free until I got back on my feet. I had no intention of going back to Gary. I didn't want to fall prey to the streets. I had the whole house to myself. I found a job working at Gottlieb Memorial Hospital in the surgical unit. My primary responsibility was prepping patients for surgery and transporting them around the hospital. The job paid about $500 every two weeks.

Within months of working, I received a call from my sister, Roxanne. She told me that Dino had gone into a rage, threatening

Orderly At Gottlieb Hospital.

the family. They left the house in a hurry, taking their belongings with them to stay at my Aunt Cynthia's house. I was furious and reached my limit; I couldn't take it anymore. All our lives, he had a way of making us fear him, and I finally had enough. He reminded me constantly when I turned 18 what he was going to do to me, and I never once forgot it. Also, all of the memories came rushing back of the day he put the gun to my head. In an emotional rage, I took off work for several days. I took the little money I had to purchase a gun. However, I discovered that in order to purchase a gun I needed to apply for an Illinois State firearms identification card. Consequently, I had to wait for a few days until my gun card arrived. Had I been able to purchase the gun that day, the outcome would have been adversely different. I was acting on pure emotion. Those few days allowed me time to think about the consequences.

My IL. State I.D. Gun Card

The gun card arrived a few days later and I bought a silver .32 semi-automatic handgun. I immediately drove home in my 1987 Grand Am in excess of 100 miles per hour with the gun in my lap. My heart was pumping so fast. I couldn't get there soon enough. Luckily, I was not pulled over by the police. I started having thoughts of me killing him so I put the gun on safety. I was afraid that if I didn't, I would kill him in an act of rage. My goal was to scare the living daylights out of him. I didn't want my mother to lose two sons; one to prison and the other one to death. When I arrived at the house, I kicked in the front door and I ran into the family room where he was sitting. He was eating a bowl of cereal, watching T.V. I grabbed his hair and put the gun to his head. I said, "Remember this? Remember when you put that gun to my head? Now get yo' stuff and get out the house!"

I told him that whatever he wanted to do I was ready. He ran to the next-door neighbor's house. My adrenaline was pumping, so I took the gun off safety and began firing in the air in broad daylight. After I let off a few rounds, the gun jammed. I wanted him to know that I meant business.

I ran into the neighbor's house and I pointed the gun at him as he crowded behind everyone. Frightened, they pleaded with me to put the gun down. I forgot the gun was off on safety as I was squeezing the trigger. The only thing that saved his life was that the gun had jammed. I could have seriously hurt or killed him right there. By this time, the police had arrived. I went outside and Dino began screaming at the officers, "This nigga trying to kill me!"

The officer on the scene happened to be a friend of mine. He asked for my gun and I handed it to him; he also asked if I had a gun permit. I showed it to him and to my surprise, he handed me back my gun. The block was packed with onlookers seeing the whole thing unfold. I told the officer about the years of abuse Dino had put my siblings and I through. I told him that I reached my breaking point. Dino couldn't believe what he was seeing. I told him to, "Pack yo' stuff up and get out of my father's house."

The officer told me to leave, but that I could return to the house the following day. Dino got his belongings out of the house and stayed at a neighbor's house. I then drove to my Aunt Cynthia's house where my mother and sister were, as if nothing happened. I didn't want my mother to worry. As I hugged my mother, the gun was tucked into the waistline of my pants. I was hoping she didn't feel it; luckily, she didn't. I told her everything would be okay and that they could return to the house within a few days. When I returned to the house the next day, I noticed Dino across the street at the neighbor's house, sitting on the porch with the shotgun he used on me years earlier between his legs. It was his way of trying to intimidate me, but I wasn't afraid anymore. I got out of the car with my gun in hand, locked and loaded. We stared each other down for a minute. I screamed out, "Whatever you try to do, I'm ready!"

He had no idea how he was preparing me for this very moment my entire life. I was fearless and was ready to die to protect my family. Ultimately the situation resolved, and we both backed down.

A few days later Roxanne and Momma returned home. I thought things would get better, but matters got even more complicated. My eldest sister Kim was there and told me about all of the horrible things Dino had done to her. My mother tried to stop her from talking but I wanted to hear more. Roxanne confided in me as well, explaining how he had been verbally and physically abusive toward her. After hearing all of these confessions, I became enraged! I felt terrible that I had not been there to protect them. My mother, angered by what they were telling me, started attacking Roxanne, pulling her hair, punching and kicking her. I got in between my mother and sister and told her to get her hands off Roxanne. I was angry and blamed my mother for all the atrocities she allowed Dino to put us through. She never held him accountable for his actions. He was allowed to do whatever he wanted to do to us. I was tired of the years of abuse and nothing being done about it. I was emotionally exhausted. The way in which my mother attacked Roxanne would mark the first time I was prepared to defend my sister against my mother. I was no longer going to allow *her* to abuse us ever again, either.

When I eventually returned to work, I got fired because I didn't get along with my supervisor. She made working conditions extremely difficult. She would give me odd jobs, like cleaning the bottom of the sink in the staff's lounge. I would get so angry I would be in tears. The day I was fired, she grabbed my shirt to get my attention and I yanked away from her. I never liked anyone putting their hands on me. She told me I was fired and called Security to escort me out the hospital. As I was changing my clothes in the locker room, I told them that if they put their hands on me they would face serious consequences. I walked out of the hospital, and they kept a safe distance behind me.

In the following weeks, I joined my brother Jamie's R&B group, Standing Room Only, as their road manager. They were just starting off so no one got paid, but it was fun to travel. I met a "friend" at the health club who would introduce me to a life of crime to make ends meet. We would return stolen merchandise to stores for large sums of cash. I was so naive that I would use my own driver's license to return the merchandise we had stolen from the store. I also kept thousands of dollars' worth of stolen merchandise in my apartment. My "friend" was good at it; he would walk into a store with nothing and leave with hundreds of dollars. On a good day, we would make as much as $2000.00 per day and divide it up between us. I didn't think about the consequences because I had been out of work for six months and needed to pay my bills. I also used the money to help my mother maintain the house in Gary.

This scam wouldn't last for long. One day, my homeboy tried to return an expensive computer, but the manager became suspicious because he didn't have the receipt. My gut instinct told me that something was about to go terribly wrong. He told the manager that he was going to the car to retrieve the receipt, but I knew that was not true because we never had receipts. I noticed that it took him a long time to return, so I went outside to see what was going on. The police had him completely surrounded. They began questioning him about the computer. I was scared beyond belief. I was sure we were going to jail, yet the police let him go. I was amazed at how easily he was able to swindle the cops. We got in the car and took off as fast as we could, leaving everything behind. That scared the living daylights out of me and I end my life of crime. I didn't want to end up in jail. My friend continued and months later got arrested. He ended up serving five years in prison. I thought about how that could have been me and was thankful for God's grace and mercy on my life. God had a plan for my life, and it was much bigger than I could have ever expected.

In 1995, I would find work in the most unlikely of places, Hull House. It would be the start of my career in serving children. Hull House was a social service agency that served youth in the Department of Children and Family Services (DCFS) transitioning into independent living. The young men on my case load came from group homes, psychiatric facilities, juvenile detention facilities and so on. As you might imagine, I had a challenging group and I was a novice. I would learn by walking through the fire. My clients placed me in life-threatening situations that could have cost me my career and safety. However, I was never afraid because Dino taught me to be fearless and I carried that attitude with me my entire life. Also, growing up in Gary made you tough. You had to learn how to survive.

In one particular incident, my client gave a drug dealer a phony twenty dollar bill to purchase marijuana; once the drug dealer found out that he had been fooled, he put a hit out on the street to have my client killed. I was afraid for my client's life when I found out this information. Chicago drug dealers were not to be taken lightly. It was all about respect. Also, calling the police would only make matters worse. Once I received this information, I set out to find this notorious drug dealer (how naive I was). I discovered that he stayed just a few blocks away from the facility where I worked. I drove to a three-flat apartment building. As I got out of my car to walk towards the apartment complex, I was confronted by several gang members seated on the porch. I asked to speak with the drug dealer and the situation became tense. As far as they knew, I was an undercover police officer. They began questioning who I was and what I wanted. I was honest with them and told them I was the advocate of the individual who had given the dealer the phony twenty-dollar bill. Fortunately, after much persuading, I was able to gain their trust. I told them that my only goal was to save my client's life and to take care of his mishandling of the "transaction." I paid them twenty dollars, with interest. They assured me they wouldn't kill him, but that they would "beat the life out of him" if they ever saw him in the neighborhood. I felt weird about that but thanked them anyway for lessening the punishment.

My clients were angry and disconnected from any sense of normalcy; however, I could definitely relate to them. I could have easily been a victim of the state because of the abuse I endured as a child. Working there would change the trajectory of my life. I discovered my passion and knew that for the rest of my life I would serve our youth. I went on to work there for four years.

Me with Min Farakhan

On October 16, 1995, I watched the inaugural Million Man March on T.V. It was on every major news network. It was a spectacular sight to see millions of black men from all over the world gathered together in peace. On that day, I chose not to go to work nor purchase anything. I wanted to join the brothers in solidarity. After listening to Minister Louis Farrakhan and other guest speakers, I begin to weep. The suffering of African Americans – in particular, the youth – had a great impact on me. From that day forward, I made a commitment to serve my community. Minister Farrakhan was in my opinion, the epitome of a man. I joined the Nation of Islam in 1996. Minister Farrakhan spoke with reverence and authority; he was not afraid to speak his mind about the atrocities that African Americans endured, and to hold the perpetrators accountable. He was a controversial figure and some saw him as a racist, but I admired his boldness. Additionally, I admired how the men embodied self-discipline, how they respected women, and how they represented themselves. I learned things about African American history that I never was taught in high school. The Nation of Islam taught me the importance of reading, so I began reading everything I could get my hands on, in particular, books about our sojourn to America. I also purchased every tape and DVD of the Minister's lectures.

My mother was furious when I joined the Nation of Islam. She was a devout Christian, and believed that every other religion was from the pits of hell. When I discussed things with her, I learned she would refute everything and tried to debate with me; however, in the Nation of Islam I was taught to never debate the truth. Some of the questions I posed to her she couldn't definitively answer. Her response most of the time was that I should never question God. I didn't like the way I was raised as a Christian because it justified the abuse I had endured my entire life. Also, my mother would take the money my father gave her to pay bills and she would pay "tithes" to crooked church organizations to support their efforts, all in the name of Jesus. We spent months without electricity and gas and it angered me. My mother was so dismayed with my decision to join the Nation of Islam that she told me, "I would rather you be like your brother Dino and a Christian than to study Islam!"

Dino had terrorized the family for decades. This further fueled my belief that I made the right choice to join the ranks of the Nation of Islam. She prayed over me as if I had joined a cult. After several years, I decided to leave the Nation of Islam because of philosophical differences, but I still maintained close relationships with brothers who I'd grown to respect and admire.

I was at a point in my life that I wanted to learn more about my father. He was a member of the Masonic Order and it had always sparked my interest. So, in 1996, I went through an initiation to become a member of Universal Lodge #65 PHA in Chicago. As a little boy, I was curious and would go through my father's belongings that he had kept hidden in the closet. I saw a black top hat, a colorful apron and white gloves. I discovered that my father was the Worshipful Master of his lodge, which is the highest-ranking position one can hold. I didn't make it that far in the ranks, but I knew his role. He was responsible for running his lodge. When I completed the initiation process, my Uncle Elmon gave me a Masonic ring. He was a Mason too, and was proud that I was able to complete the process. I was following in our family's tradition.

Masonic ring giving to me as a gift from my Uncle Elmon

My mother hated the whole idea of me becoming a Mason, of course. In her mind, I was worshiping the Devil, which was the furthest thing from the truth. At that time, I was both in the Masonic Order and studying Islam; my mother thought I had lost my mind. However, I was on a path to discover who I was, free of her influence.

Chapter 7

LOVE PRELUDE

In 1997, I met Eileen at a Bally's Total Fitness health club in Oak Park. I had watched her for weeks and was impressed with how she carried herself. She was respectful, kind, humble and courteous. One day, I mustered up enough courage to approach her and gave her my phone number. Our first "date" was on Thanksgiving. She came to my apartment and we ordered Chinese food and drank sparkling apple cider. As we began to talk, I learned that we had many things in common; among which, she told me that she was a former member of the Nation of Islam, and that she was serious about her health and wellness. As the relationship progressed, I took her to visit my family every weekend in Gary. I wanted her to have a better understanding of where I came from. Additionally, I wanted her to know my family dynamic, and the burden of responsibility I bore in taking care of them.

The first visit she accompanied me on, she was shocked. The gas was shut off in the middle of winter. The house was so cold that you could see the moisture from your breath when you talked. Several months earlier, my best friend Sean gave me several kerosene lamps to heat the house, and though they smelled really bad, they got the job done.

The house was in bad shape and when Eileen asked to use the rest room, I felt embarrassed. The bathroom door was literally off its hinges, which meant she physically had to prop the door up to close it. It was a humbling experience, but it was my reality. According to Eileen, every time I went to visit home it weighed heavily upon me, and on the rides back home I would be totally silent. I felt depressed that they were living in such terrible conditions. I didn't realize how this would impact my own relationship in years to come.

During our dating phase, which only spanned for one year, we took many walks in the park, talking about having the ideal life. We would drive to affluent neighborhoods in Oak Park and visualize living there ourselves. Sometimes we would go on the property and peek inside the homes to get a glimpse inside.

She was the most warm-spirited person I had ever met. She made a habit of thinking of others before thinking of herself. She was non-confrontational and always wanted to bring out the best in people. She carried a deep sense of humility and dignity. We became close and had an unbreakable bond. After a year of nurturing our relationship, I was convinced I wanted to marry her. She was also several weeks' pregnant and I wanted to do things right. I had never planned anything, so this would be my greatest challenge. My goal was to make it memorable. I picked her up from work in a limousine with a dozen roses and we had dinner at a nice restaurant. I told her how blessed I was to have her in my life. She had no idea what was going on. When the night came to a close, we walked to a park that was near the apartment where I lived. I sat her down on a bench and got on my knees to ask her to marry me. I told her that she was the best thing to ever happen to me, I was a better man because of her, and that I couldn't live my life without her. With tears in her eyes, she said, "Yes." I felt like the luckiest man in the world.

On May 8, 1999, Eileen and I got married. She was 6 months pregnant with our first son, Michael. Eileen's sisters did a beautiful job planning the wedding. However, minutes before the ceremony, I had an emotional breakdown. The grief and pain of my father's absence hit me like a ton of bricks. I wish he could've been there to see the man that I had become. I cried profusely. I literally had to be held up by my brothers. I realized then that I had not properly allowed myself to grieve. I struggled, but eventually gathered myself together in time for the wedding ceremony. For most of the wedding, my eyes were red from crying. My brother Rodney was my best man and he helped me get through it. We had an awesome time. Jamie read a poem, my family sang – we danced and partied the night away.

Three months later (August 27th, 1999), Michael Jr. was born. It was one of the proudest, most soul-transforming moments of my life. He was my namesake. By this time, Eileen and I had moved to a large one-bedroom apartment in Oak Park. I cleaned the apartment from top to bottom to make sure it was clean when they arrived home. The entire apartment smelled like bleach. On Mike Jr.'s first day home, I hovered over his crib staring at him and started crying. I was overcome with emotion. I couldn't believe I was responsible for this child and that he would depend on me for everything. I begin to ask God for guidance to raise him the way He saw fit. I didn't want him growing up experiencing the trauma I had survived. The love I had for him was overwhelming, and would change my life. I would drive him around through poverty-stricken neighborhoods as an infant. I would tell him that my goal for his life was for him to be a servant to the poor. I wanted that realization and mission to pierce his small soul.

I worked two jobs and was enrolled at Northeastern Illinois University, in the School of Psychology program, to get my bachelor's degree. I wanted to make sure I could provide for my family. It was a difficult time and money was tight. As you can imagine, we struggled as new parents; however, Eileen and I made sure that Mike Jr.'s needs were met.

Because I worked two jobs and was in school, I didn't make it home until 11:30 P.M. However, Michael seemed to always know when I came home. He was ready to play, and after a few minutes of playtime, I would sit him down on my lap at the computer as I completed my homework. He was my motivation to do my very best. One of the reasons I studied psychology was to understand the dysfunction in my family life and childhood. I had a deep yearning to understand the depression and its origin that ran rampant in my family.

I had worked at a number of psychiatric facilities and assumed that the classwork would be easy. However, that was not the case at all. I signed up to receive tutoring because I needed all the support I could get.

Two weeks before I was expected to turn in my thesis to the graduation panel, I received numerous phone calls from family members about issues they were having, which all required my help. I had always been there for my family, but this time was different. I had my own family now, and my top priority was them. In order to eliminate distractions, I cut the phone line so that I could focus all my attention on my coursework.

Through God's grace, I finished my thesis and met in front of a panel of advisors from the Psychology Department. They asked me numerous questions about my learning experience and tested my empirical knowledge. I responded the best I could. After, they asked me to step outside so they could discuss matters with each other. It felt like the longest wait of my life. Within minutes, they asked me to return. They unanimously agreed to reward me with a Bachelor's in Psychological and Behavioral Studies in Adolescents. I was filled with gratitude and thanked each of them for their support throughout the program. I sat down in the hall and cried tears of joy. I thought about the tumultuous journey I withstood, and through it all, finished. I had promised my father that I would graduate from college. I promised my wife and newborn son that I would never quit. I was proud that I was able to make good on my promise. I was sure my father was proud of me.

The plan was set for me to graduate; however, in order to do so, Northeastern Illinois University required graduates to pass a writing exam. Upon taking it, I failed twice. I was frustrated, so I signed up for tutoring. Thankfully, my tutor was patient and taught me the science of writing. She taught me how to construct paragraphs, and how I should read the last sentence first when I completed writing assignments. I remember this vividly because it literally changed my writing style over night. I was able to catch mistakes more easily. She was able to teach me how I learned best. I started to write more clearly, and my thoughts flowed effortlessly. I was so thankful for her dedication and commitment to ensuring that I was prepared. Her dedication and commitment reaped dividends, and needless to say, I passed! I was overjoyed. I never got a chance to thank her. I hope one day for an opportunity to tell her just how much she meant to me. The entire process taught me a valuable lesson; life will only give you what you are willing to sacrifice. I had to put in the hours of hard work.

For me, it was much more than a degree. It was about putting myself in the position to provide for Eileen and Michael Jr. I carried that intense drive and work ethic with me into my career in education, for better and for worse.

Chapter 8

❖

McGrone the Renegade

In 2001, I accepted a job at West Town Academy Alternative School. I taught African American history and also worked with youth in the Department of Children and Family Services (DCFS). The school was located in a dangerous community, however, many of the students enrolled in West Town Academy were expelled Chicago Public School (CPS) students and were seeking a second chance. I once had a student to tell me he was "Hot" which meant that he brought a gun to school. He said the neighborhood where he lived, the gangs were at war and he wanted to protect himself. At any other school, he would have been arrested and expelled; however, you had to understand what students like him were going through. You had to use commons sense, this was not a dangerous student, in fact, he was really smart and a gifted rapper. A few times while taking him home, I saw where he lived, and my thoughts were that if I lived in this neighborhood, I would try to protect myself too. You could feel the tension in the air. I could tell something was not right. By no means am I advocating for students to carry weapons to school, however, this was his way of protecting himself from the violence in his community and to make sure he got home safe. As time progressed, I had many unique encounters with students and residents in the community. This was the origin of me learning about the demographics of the community, so I made it my personal business to walk students home to ensure they made it home safely. However, I was a tough teacher and didn't allow students to come to my class late. My stringent attitude was because I knew the odds were stacked against them. I NEVER allowed them to make excuses.

I was well-prepared to deliver quality instruction and wasted no time. If a student came to my class late, I required them to stand until I told them they could sit down. One particular incident comes to mind – a student arrived late to my classroom and I had him stand up until I gave him permission to sit down. After a while, he got dizzy and passed out. I sent a student to the cafeteria to get some orange juice to revive him. After a couple of sips, the student regained his equilibrium, so I required him to continue standing. The students thought I was crazy but I was not one to play with. I wanted them to understand that my time was valuable and that I was serious about their education.

Me with Chairman Fred Hampton

When we read books, I had them research the author. I never wanted my students to believe everything they read. I wanted them to read between the lines and to question everything. Though they could be a challenge, they were highly intelligent and engaged. I allowed them to be themselves, and the discussions we had in class were deep and thoughtful. I wanted them to challenge me, contrary to how students are customarily taught in today's educational system. I believe they taught me more than I could've ever taught them. We had dynamic speakers come in that they could relate to. The conversations were electrifying. In one chapter of our reading, we covered the Black Panther Party. I knew Chairman Fred Hampton Jr., the son of the late Chairman Fred Hampton Sr. (president of the Chicago chapter of the Black Panthers), so I invited him to come talk with my students. The students were excited; however, the school director thought it would be too controversial to bring him in. I assured her that was not the case at all. She still refused. The students were prepared to walk out if their demands weren't met. Eventually, she relented and the students got the experience of a lifetime. We all learned a great deal. I gave them assignments they valued. This particular assignment I explained to them how to write out their family tree. The goal was for them was to learn as much about their family they could. They had to come up with a list of questions. The students were excited to get the project underway. However, it would be more difficult than they realized. For this assignment they would have to interview members of their family. Many of them refused

Herbert, poet

to divulge any personal information. I instructed the students to communicate to their families that this assignment was not for my indulgence but to help them avoid certain historical pitfalls. From then on they were better received. My challenge though came when I told students to complete the assignment using symbols to indicate family members and color codes. I didn't allow them any room to be creative and Herbert refused to do the assignment and I was prepared to fail him. He suggested a more creative way of doing it. Herbert was a gifted poet and I reluctantly agreed. I didn't know how he was going to do it, but I would be proven wrong, He was excited and took ownership because I was working with how he learned. At the completion of the project, the students did an exceptional job. Herbert produced a masterpiece. He talked about his family's history using poetry. He had us all mesmerized. It was genius! He met the goal. It is at that time I realized the importance of differentiation in your instruction. I learned that when you can teach children how they learn you can better prepare them for life.

My class was diverse and Dianna would be the first gay student I taught. She was tough and was not to be played with. She was a member of the Black Stone gang and was banned from all Chicago Public Schools (CPS). She proudly wore black and red to represent the colors of the Stones. Her and I instantly clicked because she was a revolutionary and loved to read. At first glance, you would never see her as being intelligent. Dianna wore baggy clothes and kept a low haircut. However, when she spoke you knew she was something special. She was articulate and spoke with passion. She loved to read especially books about history. She would be the first student to give me books to read. She would challenge me in the classroom, so I know I had to bring my "A" game. She raised the level of expectation and made class fun. She and I become good friends.

One day, Dianna called with the most devastating news I had ever heard. She was crying uncontrollably; I had to calm her down. She told me while she was at home her parents got into a bad argument. Her father retrieved his gun and was aiming it at her mother. She was pleading with him to put it down. She was trying to keep him from shooting her mother, when she felt the bullets whisk pass her face. She said he eventually was able to fire multiple rounds killing her mom, and by the time the police had totally surrounded the house, her father committed suicide right in front of her. I was numb; all I could do was listen. I didn't have the words to say. All I could do was just be there for her. In the coming days, Dianna would be responsible for arranging 2 funerals on the same day. She is by far one of the strongest individuals I'd ever met. Life knocked her to the very core, however, she uses her pain to spread a message of hope and love. Now, Dianna is a well known Chicago spoken word artist and writes plays.

Dianna, spoken word artist

Principal Michael McGrone Sr.

My class was full of talented and amazing students and Mercedes was one of them. However, she was a student not to be played with. She didn't care who she fought male or female. She was definitely an alpha female and ruled with an iron fist. She had an aura about her. Everything she did she did it with confidence. She was a gifted rapper and could rap circles around the best of them. When she rhymed she came from the top of her head; she didn't write down anything. To this day, I have never heard a female rapper who was better and I'm making reference to those in the rap industry as well. After class, guys would challenge her and one by one she would desecrate them using their own words against them. Mercedes still raps to this day and is a successful realtor.

Me with Willie Lloyd "King of Kings" of the Vice Lord Nation

The following year, a student introduced me to the infamous Willie Lloyd, the King of Kings of the Vice Lord Nation. He wanted to meet me after hearing about the great work I was doing in the community. I was shocked! Willie was starting an origination called "Against All Odds "and wanted me to be part of it. The goal of the origination was to stop the violence in the streets of Chicago and to discourage young men from joining gangs and pursue their education. I would be responsible for convincing teenage gang members to go back to school. I'd always heard stories about how dangerous he was and how he was feared by many. In my mind he was this larger-than-life figure. However, when I finally met him for the first time, he stood only about 5'7" and weighed just under 155 pounds. I didn't see him as this notorious gang leader that everyone spoke of. But as time went on, I would learn just how dangerous his past meant to those in the community. I attended meetings he held on the West Side of Chicago every Thursday. I met with fearless leaders like Chairman Fred (leader of the Chicago Black Panthers), Bennie Lee (former leader of the Conservative Vice Lords; mentor and teacher at Northeastern IL Univ.), Aron Patterson (a high-ranking Black Stone member), "Big Moss" (leader of the South Side Black Stones), "King Troy" (leader of the Mafia Insane Vice Lords) and "Zoom" (Black Stone Leader) and other gang leaders in Chicago. It was fascinating listening to their stories. In one meeting, Willie informed us that our cell phones had been tapped and that our conversations were being recorded. I didn't understand – however, when he provided examples of the echo sounds emanating from our cell phones, it was evident that our cell phones were, in fact, being infiltrated. When we finished our meetings, helicopters could be seen hovering over and plain-clothes police officers could be seen watching our every move. It was then that I knew just how notorious the company of people I was in. It was a scene out of a movie. I was exposed to street life on a whole new level. Some of the gang leaders I met were killers. They cared nothing about taking your life and I was considered an outsider.

King Troy was not too friendly and was not to be trifled with. He even questioned Willie (in my presence) as to why I was there. When I attempted to engage him in conversation he said, "Don't say anything to me," and stared me down. It would be the first time I felt a true fear of another human being. I knew he could kill me, or have me killed, and think nothing of it. However, because of Willie, I gained protection through association.

After weeks of attending the meetings, Willie encouraged me to accept the vice president position for "Against All Odds". It was a great privilege because my heart was always to save our youth. I was voted in by the board of directors. Mr. Willis, an attorney, served as the President and was the brains behind the operation.

Principal Michael McGrone Sr.

We worked closely with Mr. Hardiman who was the director of Cease Fire. He along with former gang members and street activist went into the communities and collaborate with current gang members to stop the violence. Cease Fire was successful in part because of the support they received from Willie and other gang leaders in the group. I witnessed Willie, on several phone conversations, negotiate with gang leaders to stop the violence. He still had great influence and power. Sometimes we would go for walks, and I would learn just how violent his past was.

One particular day, I walked with him to a clothing store on the West Side of Chicago, and everyone ran and locked themselves in a back room. He had to convince them that he was not the Willie of the past, and that he was trying to make the community safer. This was shocking to me, and made me realize just how dangerous he really was. He shared intimate details about his life with me. He said he never wanted to be King of the Vice Lords, but instead he aspired to be the War Counselor, because he loved fighting. He explained that the "Unknown Vice Lords" got their name from the police because every time they would investigate crimes committed by them they would put down on reports the assailant was labeled as "Unknown." He also explained that in the early days, he, along with fellow gang members, would drive around the neighborhood referred to as the "Holy City" in a black truck that looked like a U-Haul, and would terrorize the community. He said that he spent most of his life in and out of prison. He said that he had done a lot of bad things in his life, and that if he died a horrible death, he would have to accept it as karma. He understood that whatever you sow, you shall reap. His words would prove to be prophetic in months to come.

He was impressed by the love and respect my students showed me. This intrigued him because I was leading them in the right direction. I actually got him to come to West Town Academy to talk to my students. When he traveled, I thought he would have an entourage; instead, he traveled with a pink-eyed, albino pit bull he called "White Boy. My students were beyond amazed that I had that type of influence where I could invite one of Chicago's most notorious gang leaders to the school. It was quite an interesting experience, having him talk to my students about the history of gangs in Chicago and how he came through the ranks. My students had heard about him but never knew him personally. They got a chance to ask him questions about his life and what made him change. He was brutally honest. I also invited Benney Lee, former leader of the Conservative Vice Lords to talk to the students. At the age of 13, he was the youngest person to ever lead the gang. Benny spent most of his life in and out of jail and even spent time on death row for participating in a riot at Pontiac Prison. He is now a mentor and a former Northeastern IL. University professor. Though Willie and I spent countless hours together, I never knew the violent person he was portrayed to be. The Willie I met was beginning to understand that the life he created was all deception, and he wanted to correct his wrongs.

Me with Benny Lee former leader of the Conservative Vice Lords

Principal Michael McGrone Sr.

All I knew was that he loved flowers and children. When my son Jeremiah was born on April 12, 2003, he came to the hospital, accompanied by his wife, Willa, to bring Eileen a bouquet of flowers and to give us their blessings. When Eileen asked who he was, I told her Willie Lloyd. She was absolutely shocked! One of the most notorious gang members in Chicago's history brought her a bouquet of flowers. He took pictures holding my son. In an unconventional way, he became part of the family. I went as far as inviting every gang leader in Chicago I knew to my house in South Holland, to discuss ways we could improve the community by coming up with strategic methods to stop the violence. My friends couldn't believe how well-respected I was among the gang leadership in Chicago, but were pleasantly surprised when they saw the group for themselves up close and personal at my home.

In August of 2003, I received a call that Willie had been shot. He was walking his pit bull in Garfield Park on the West Side of Chicago, when several gunmen approached him and started shooting point blank. Somehow he survived, but as expected, he was in grave condition. Because he was a former gang leader, the *Chicago Tribune* featured him on the front page of the newspaper. It was big news because Willie was one of the last-known original gang leaders that were alive and not in jail. Mayor Daley was furious that the *Chicago Tribune* gave the case such media attention, because Willie had been known as a cop killer. Word of the shooting spread quickly throughout Chicago. Every gang faction in the city was at the hospital. Willie survived the shooting but was left a quadriplegic. After that incident, I never saw Willie again. He passed away in July of 2015 at the age of 64. Working with him was truly a transformative experience. I learned who he was as a man, about street life (on a whole new level), his demons and how to navigate the street.

Me to the far right leading a march for political prisoners

Shortly after Willie's shooting, I got involved in community activism. I marched for political prisoners and attended rallies. I also led marches and hosted other community initiatives. Studying the atrocities of what African Americans went through, I wanted freedom, justice, and equality for my people, and I was willing to gain it at any cost. My attitude was intimidating to most people, especially in the workplace. I never stayed on a job for more than a year. This concerned Eileen because every year I was searching for a new job. I had to get serious. I understood why she was nervous. She wanted stability.

In 2007, I accepted a position at Youth Connection Leadership Academy as the Dean of Students. It would become a transformative experience in my development as a leader in school culture. Here I was once again, working with students who had dropped out of school, and all they wanted was a second chance. The students came in with various social and emotional issues. They were angry and lacked self-motivation.

Though they wanted better for themselves, they did not have the tools or mentorship to make that happen. Suspensions were high and the morale among the students was low. This gave me the opportunity to come up with something creative to revolutionize the school.

Orientation for boys mentoring program at YCLA

First, I wrote a school creed with a positive affirmation, which I required students to recite each morning. The intent was to give the students a sense of purpose and direction. After a while, the students owned it and began to look forward to starting their day with it. They came ready to learn. Because the boys were the lowest academic performers and had the most discipline problems, I started what would be my first boys' mentoring program, called Men of Distinction. I required no criteria to join because I wanted to give everyone a fair chance. We started off with 21 candidates. I told them the process would be grueling and intense, and that most likely, more than half of them would quit before it was over. I used this challenging strategy because I knew it would challenge their ego and increase participation. Weeks later, I had an orientation with the parents to let them know about the program and what role they would play in it. I also introduced them to the facilitators who would be working with me throughout the duration of the program.

My first session with the young men

Our first meeting took place on a Sunday. It was cold and rainy. The boys came dressed in white t-shirts and jeans, which I had required. I let them know that this would be a tough journey. We talked about expectations and the true essence of brotherhood. The meeting lasted for several hours, and at one point they got hungry. The only thing I had to feed them was a couple of bags of oranges, which they didn't want. I didn't have a budget at the time, but I was not going to allow that to deter me from working with young men who were desperately searching for guidance. My philosophy was that God would supply all my needs because my heart was in the right place. Nonetheless, I allowed them to go to McDonald's as a group. The neighborhood was heavily saturated with gangs, so I begin to worry because it took them a while to return. Soon there after, one by one, they began to stroll in. Their clothes were soaking wet from the rain and they were breathing heavily. Their clothes were also stretched out of shape.

I was confused and asked them what happened. They explained that they got into a fight with local gang members. They said one of the young men got hit by a car trying to escape but did not get hurt. They reported that the car actually stopped and he ran into it. When they all returned some of them were crying, but most of them were furious and wanted to retaliate in other, aggressive ways. Opposed to letting them go home, I kept them there to continue the process. I used the incident to teach them life lessons. They thought I was crazy. I talked about how poverty and gangs were a byproduct of family dysfunction, and that they were caught up in the matrix. Some of them were experts on the topic because they were active gang members themselves. That day they realized just how serious I was. This would be my mindset throughout the duration of the program. No excuses! I was intense. We met practically every day (after school) and on the weekends. I had them marching in the middle of the winter and got angry if they complained it was cold. I put them in stressful situations on purpose as a metaphor for life. I wanted them to understand that success came at a price. Essentially what I was teaching came from my own life experiences. I constantly reminded them that the world doesn't owe you anything.

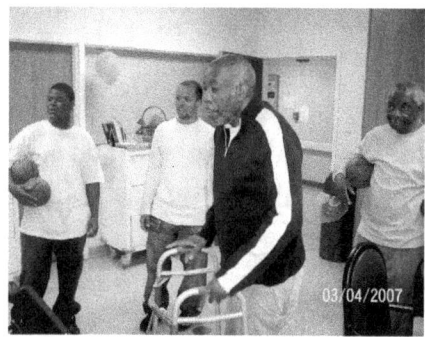 

MOD Entertaining Bronzeville residence   MOD playing games with Bronzeville residents

I was fortunate enough to partner with the Bronzeville nursing home that was located just a few blocks away from the school. I wanted to teach the young men the value of community service but more importantly, how valuable the elderly are to our history and our survival. We met there several times a week to play games, setting out hops that mimic the men of Omega Phi Fraternity Inc. and talked to them. The young men learned a great deal. The elders became their surrogate parents. We did whatever we could do to add value to their lives. Some of the residents didn't have family visits, so we adopted them as our own family members and spent additional time with them, especially on holidays. As a part of our creed, I wanted the young men to understand that the only way to achieve true happiness is by serving others, and we did it with pride!

At the conclusion of the program, five young men survived the rigorous process. They were fitted with custom blazers, prepared speeches and practiced the "hops" they learned from the hop-master himself, Mr. Edwards of Omega Psi Phi Fraternity Inc.

On March 30th, it was their time to shine. I had hired a live band, also residents from Bronzeville and the entire student body were in attendance. The show was spectacular, and the attendees were

Men Of Distinction Closing Ceremony

inspired by what the young men were able to accomplish. At the conclusion of the ceremony, I was proud to announce their names and put their blazers on them that they had worked so hard for. After, I allowed all of the young men who participated in the program to be recognized as well. They were all dressed to impress. I was grateful for the support I received from the Youth Charter Connection Schools (YCCS) administration and the individuals who sacrificed their time to support me in this initiative. This program would serve as a blueprint for programs I would facilitate in the future.

Men of Distinction

More than anything else, the greatest success of the Men of Distinction program was that it changed the culture of the school. Every student wanted to be a part of the group after that. However, I only stayed at Youth Connection Leadership Academy for one year before leaving for my next assignment.

Chapter 9

❖

RITES OF PASSAGE

By the summer of 2007, I was hired at ACE Technical Charter High School (or "ACE Tech") as the Dean of Students. ACE Tech was in its fourth year of existence and would soon be graduating its first class. ACE had serious student climate and culture issues. There were numerous fights on and off-campus. 390 students were suspended in the previous year, and the total enrollment was just under 600. To make matters even more serious, ACE Tech was located in Englewood, which was considered one of the most dangerous communities in Chicago. However, the students who attended ACE Tech came from all over the city. This would be more challenging than I ever could have expected because the community did not embrace these students.

My first week as the Dean of Students, I noticed that the students rarely had any regard for the rules. Quite a few of them arrived to school late with no sense of urgency to get to class whatsoever. It bothered me that this was the normalized culture. There was no accountability. Students would get to know me fairly quickly. I went right to work and came up with an "outside the box" strategy to minimize tardiness. Students who came to school late had to write messages on poster boards that read inspirational statements like," We love our community," "Children need their fathers," and "We are the future leaders." They had no idea what they were writing them for; soon they would be in for a surprise of their lives. I led groups as large as thirty students as we would walk up and down 55th Street. To make sure they heard me loud and clear, I used a megaphone. This helped me keep them orderly because I required them to walk in a single file line. I made it clear that if they couldn't maintain a straight line I would have them walk for an even longer distance and in most cases, it was miles. Needless to say, they kept the line straight and if they saw a peer get out of line, they quickly redirected them. They knew I was not playing. As we would walk, people would blow their horns in support of what I was doing. On several occasions, we even had police escorts. Because I had so many students at the time, it became a spectacle. Some students were so embarrassed that they never came late to school again. I did this every single day, and within the first three months cut tardiness by 90%.

Me walking with students down 55th St. who arrived late to school

I have always believed in using consequences to teach. On this particular day, two Latino male students came to school wearing black and gold to represent their gang, the Latin Kings. The Latin Kings are primarily located in the Humboldt Park community in Chicago. I confronted these young men and told them how they were placing themselves in a dangerous situation that threatened their lives. ACE Tech was located in a community that was heavily populated with Gangster Disciples (GD's), whose colors were royal blue and black. These opposing gangs hated each other. The young men insisted that they were not afraid and could handle anything that they were confronted with. Being the devil's advocate I was, I wanted to call their bluff. Unbeknownst to them, I was well respected among the leaders of the Gangster Disciples (GD's).

I came up with a plan to frighten the hell out of them. I met with the leaders of the GD's and told them to scare the living daylight out of them. I wanted them to understand that "thug life" was nothing to play with. I explained to them that they were kids and did not understand the severity of their behavior. I walked them to the corner of 55th and State and had them wait there for a few minutes as they mingled with one another. They told me they were prepared for whatever came their way. I replied "Okay," and walked away. They had no idea what was about to happen next.

Within seconds, they were completely surrounded by approximately thirty members of the Gangster Disciples, and I was in the nearby Kentucky Fried Chicken (KFC) watching the whole encounter unfold. I knew they wouldn't get hurt, but I wanted to teach them a valuable life lesson. Members of the Gangster Disciples made them take off their shirts in broad daylight and got into their faces, threatening them. They then lured them to a nearby field to pay a hefty price. Once it was evident that they had learned their lesson, I approached the scene. I made it a teachable moment. I talked about choices. Members of the GD's also shared pearls of wisdom. It was truly a sight to see the boys being taught about street life in its rawest form. The young men were relieved I was able to come to their aid. They were scared straight and were taught a valuable lesson. They ended up becoming friends with the GD's. What I've learned about working with hardcore gang members is that nothing can compare to establishing positive relationships. It was important to me to build bridges in the community, making it more difficult for the gang to perceive the students as a threat. My thought is that it's hard to fight someone you know, love and respect.

Using consequences to teach has been a major theme throughout my career as an educator. With that being said, I found out that a group of my students at ACE Tech were caught stealing at a nearby gas station. I was furious! The students had a reputation for being a nuisance in the community and my goal was to change that. I went to the gas station and was able to review the video footage. The students all rushed into the store at one time and stole whatever they could get their hands on. I came up with a plan to resolve the problem. I rounded up all of the guys who were involved. We went back to the store to apologize to the owner. We also cleaned up his property. He supplied us with brooms and bags. I had them picking up trash and sweeping the entire property. As the young men cleaned, I talked with them about peer pressure and making good choices. They then felt remorse for what they had done. When we returned to the store after cleaning outside, the boys apologized again for their actions. To our surprise, the store manager offered them free drinks. At first I was reluctant to reward the students because of what they had done, but the store manager insisted. They all shook his hand and learned a great lesson. I was elated because I was able to teach the young men about valuing the community they live in and creating positive relationships. I didn't want them to be viewed as a threat.

I saw great potential at ACE Tech and wanted to start a rite of passage program for the senior class. I consulted with my cousin Darryl and my business associate, Willie. I also brought in other individuals I worked with in the past to assist in the process. The name of our consulting group was called MTL (Mentoring Tomorrow's Leaders). We worked to put an entire program together that would take approximately three months for the students to complete. The program also involved the students' parents. We had an orientation with the parents and students, which was well attended. We informed them that the process would be a spiritual journey. We didn't have specific eligibility criteria because we wanted to give every student an equal opportunity to participate. When we started the program, everyone was given instructions: academic expectations, what to wear, proper conduct, community service projects, and what the program would entail. We met every day after school until 7 P.M. and as late as 9 P.M. Some students could not handle the intense schedule and would end up quitting. I was not concerned about the dwindling numbers, but rather maintaining the integrity of the program. Those students who were able to endure the intensity of the program became even closer with each other. We were able to provide social and emotional support for many of the problems they had encountered throughout their life. Students became each other's source of strength, and were able to share detailed experiences as to what they went through.

We had numerous breakthroughs. Most of our sessions took place in Room 209. A lot of lives were transformed in that small room. I used various unorthodox methods to get students to talk about the trauma they experienced. I confronted them dead-on many times, risking my own health and safety. My goal was to get them to let go of the past and to live in the moment. I called it "emotional purging." A true example of "purging" would be displayed on this day with a program participant named Reggie. I was angry on this particular day. The students were not taking the program seriously and were becoming complacent. I went off on them. I reminded them of the sacrifices that I, as well as my team, were making to ensure that they successfully completed the program. I focused my attention on Rodney. He rarely spoke and walked around with his head down. This bothered me because I saw greatness in him. The students knew him well because he was homeless; however, I didn't care. I wanted him to "man up." I had been homeless too, and never used it as an excuse. I told him that the world owes you nothing, and that he should stop feeling sorry for himself. As I continued to focus my attention on Rodney, I noticed Reggie from across the room getting more and more agitated. He asked me why was I "bullying" Rodney. He told me to leave him alone. I ask him why was he so concerned about me "bullying" Rodney and he sharply replied, "Because I hate bullies."

He explained how hard his life was and how he was bullied as a child. I wanted to use this opportunity to get him to elaborate more. Somehow this situation was not about Rodney and more about him dealing with his own feelings of insecurity. The heated exchange between Reggie and I made some students nervous, while others started crying. I told him I didn't care about his "lil" life because his life couldn't compare to mine! He was furious and jumped out of his seat, stalking toward me in an aggressive manner. The young men in the classroom got in between us, fearing that he would attack me. However, I remained calm, clasping my hands behind my back so that he didn't feel threatened. He was pushing his peers back, stating that he was not going to attack me, that he just wanted to get his point across. I told him that even if he tried to punch me, I wouldn't hit him back because the fight was not about me. He eventually returned to his seat. I started questioning him as to what triggered him to respond so violently. I ask if it had anything thing to do with his father and he said, "Maybe." I knew this was the underlying issue. He said that his father's release date from prison was approaching soon and that he was getting anxious. Fortunately, I was able to allay his anxiety. I told him I would be there with him every step of the way when his father was released from prison.

Reggie was known for his ability to fight and would never back down from anyone. There was nothing I could do to get him to change his behavior. This is how he coped with stored-up aggression. He fought his way through life. The fights he was involved in were never one-on-one, but instead involved multiple individuals – and he won most of them. I would tell Reggie that one day he was going to make a lot of money fighting. He also came to school high, often reeking of marijuana. I would talk to him for hours about how marijuana was a gateway for more potent drugs for most individuals; however, he stated that he would never get caught up in that. In the years following, I had no idea how prophetic my words would be. Today, Reggie is a professional MMA (Mix Martial Arts) fighter. He takes his art seriously and he is drug-free. He pushed through his greatest pains. I am proud of the man he has become, as he's continued to grow and evolve.

Reggie MMA Champion

The students in the program ranged from 17 to 19 years of age. Emotionally, they were stunted because of the trauma they experienced, and their chronological age did not align with their emotional age. This would be a complex and sensitive journey. They would confide in me their innermost secrets. Many times I cried (in seclusion) because the stories they shared with me would remind me of my own childhood trauma that I repressed for years. In order to help them I would have to let go of the past as well. I would end up becoming a program participant too, in a way. The program I founded was helping me come to grips with my own demons.

The moment the students let go of their pain

At the conclusion of the program, I had the students complete several exercises, one of which would challenge them to their very cores. I had the students sit in a circle. It was a grey day. The room had a stillness about it and the somber tone was set. I was always a stickler about the atmosphere being right before we would start sessions. Students knew I did not tolerate any laughing, joking, or playing. It was a distraction and could alter the flow of the meeting. Nonetheless, the day couldn't have been better. I required students to write down things in their life they hadn't shared with anybody. I passed out a sheet of paper and gave students the instructions. The room was still; the students did not utter a word. You could feel the emotion consuming the room; students were sniffling and wiping the tears away. Once they finished writing what they had gone through, they tore the papers into small pieces. I walked around the room with a tin can for each of them to discard the papers. I hugged each student as tears streamed down their faces. For some, this was one of the most emotional experiences they had ever gone through. There was not a dry eye left in the room.

This activity was particularly transformative for Rodney. He had a very tumultuous childhood. He spent 12 years in foster care, his parents were drug addicts, he was displaced from his siblings and labeled Special Ed, and he spent most of his senior year living in homeless shelters. He was the last one to complete the activity. It was obvious that he was reliving the traumatic events he had endured. He was crying profusely and I went over to hug him. I told him that for as long as it took him to complete the activity, I wouldn't leave his side. He was so emotional that the pressure he applied to the paper began to rip it apart; however, he continued writing. When he finished, he decided to keep what he had written as a reminder as to just how far he'd come.

After, we went outside and stood in a circle with our arms interlocked with each other. I placed the can on the ground in the middle of the circle. I told the students that this act would be symbolic of releasing the pain that they had suffered their entire life: physical and sexual abuse, broken promises, shattered dreams, abandonment, misery, and many more unfortunate events. I took a lighter and set the paper on fire. As the paper burned, they all stood in silence, thinking about all of the ways they would commit to a better life going forward. When the fire became dim, it officially marked the end of the Rites of Passage program, and from that moment on, the group was known as the first "ACE Tech Ambassadors." They all erupted in celebration, hugging one another in gratitude and expressing how they overcame extreme obstacles to complete the process. I was truly proud of them. Unbeknownst to them, I had completed the process as well.

After the celebration, I had a camera placed in a room to record the students speaking to their future selves. The objective was for them to talk about their hopes and dreams and about the kind of life they wanted for their children. It was a very powerful exercise. Many of them emerged from the room crying, overwhelmed with emotion. It's been over 10 years and none of them have yet seen themselves in the video. When the moment finally arrives, I'm sure it will be an emotional journey for both them and me.

ACE Tech Ambassadors

Over the next month, my team and I worked with the students to prepare for their culminating activity, which would take place at the South Shore Cultural Center. They had to recite poems, share their experiences, and do a step show, which they would perform in front of their parents, friends, teachers, and administrators. We practiced in the afternoons and on the weekends, and on the day of the ceremony the dedicated practice time paid off. It was a grand celebration. I thanked everyone who helped make the Rites of Passage program a success. They had sacrificed their time, money and expertise. The Class of 2008 ACE Tech Ambassadors were a special group of students and will live in my heart forever. I'm proud of the individuals they have become.

Chapter 10

PAYING THE PRICE

One of my mentors would always say to me, "With great success comes great sacrifice." It wouldn't be long before I'd learn what that meant when I dealt with a life-changing experience that would almost cost me my own life. My fearless, tireless, and ambitious work with the Men of Distinction and the ACE Tech Ambassadors did not come without its repercussions. I was terminated from ACE Tech because my strategies were not always understood. I always believed that schools should be a refuge for the community. At ACE Tech, I had invited gang members into the school to have open gym on

Me mentoring boys at ACE TEch.

the weekends; it wasn't about basketball per say, but building a relationship with the community. I also invited the homeless into the gym, where the students would prepare hot meals for them. I also required the students to eat with them. I took the students out into the community to meet with rival gang factions, in an effort to create peace and reconciliation within the community. I invited students to my home on the weekends for mentoring sessions. I spent my lunch breaks traveling to a nearby crack house to feed the homeless with leftover food from lunch. I did not worry about my safety because I had gained a trusting relationship with the people in the community. I became a dependable resource, and I did it all with pride. Nothing was off-limits for me. I remember being at my lowest and God comforting me in the stillness in the night. It often brings me to tears when I think about staring death in the face and surviving. Helping people is my way of thanking God for His blessings and mercy on my life.

"Momma Netty" was homeless and was caring for her grandson whose mother was incarcerated. She lived in a crack house. As you might imagine, it was not a safe environment for any child to live in. I was curious as to why he was not in school and wanted to help her get him back in school. Additionally, he didn't have adequate clothes, so I bought clothes for him and would cut his hair so he would look presentable. I also did what I could to help her find housing. On this particular day, I was summoned to the main office. There Momma Netty stood, crying, saying that her husband had died. I was confused because I never even knew she was married. They lived a complex and separate life, but she still loved him. His body was housed in the Cook County's morgue for days because she did not have the money to have a funeral. I did research and discovered he was an army veteran. Therefore, I was able to secure funds for him to have a proper burial. I took care of everything; all Momma Netty had to do was show up at the funeral. I transported the whole family in my truck. It was filled to capacity. The funeral home was gracious and made sure everything went effortlessly. Momma Netty was most appreciative and I was privileged to be there for her, just as others have been supportive of me. Later, I took the family out to eat and we had a great time socializing. This act provided me with legendary status among the people in the community. Word spread fast and I was embraced even more. I would walk through the neighborhood and they would scream out the window, "Dean McGrone is here!" It felt good. They were like family. I would treat them to KFC as they talked to me about the issues they were facing in the community. I gained valuable insight on how to help the neighborhood and its residents.

I would have fundraisers to help out the poor that were led by the students. We also gave away clothes and served hot meals. The goal was to teach students about humanity and unselfish living.

I became good friends with a local drug addict named Bay Bay. She and I met at the local KFC, where I spent most of my lunch breaks. When I ordered my chicken, there was a song playing called "A Bay Bay." To my surprise, Bay Bay started dancing close behind me. The fast food restaurant was filled with members of the community who knew Bay Bay, who started laughing. She was well-loved, despite her drug addiction. Rather than become agitated by what she was doing, I turned around and started dancing with her, right then and there. We were getting down! The onlookers in the restaurant thought it was hilarious. After

The Twists & Turns of Possibility

Me and Bay Bay

that, we developed a special bond. I even made her my valentine for Valentine's Day. I bought her a dozen roses and brought her to the school as I held her hand. I wanted her to feel special. I also wanted to teach the students about humanity and acts of kindness. Bay Bay lived a hard life. She frequented crack houses and begged for money to support her drug habit. Due to her substance abuse, she had a very hard exterior and she was always mistaken for a man. She wore baggy men's clothes, her hair was cut low, her hands and arms were swollen from the drug needles and her teeth were decayed or missing. One day, she came to my office in tears. She said that some of my students were taunting her, making fun of the fact that she was a struggling drug addict and homeless. I was furious! I gathered the entire student body in the gymnasium so that Bay Bay could tell her story. She told the students how attractive she used to be, but through a series of bad choices she veered down the wrong path. She started using marijuana and soon went on to abuse heroin. To support her drug

Me with Bay Bay on 55th and State

habit, she started prostituting on the street. As a result, she had 10 children, of whom she does not know who most of their fathers are, because she got pregnant while serving "Johns." She said that all of her children are wards of the state. She also said that she had been beaten, raped and left for dead. At the completion of Bay Bay's emotional testimony, all of the students lined up to give her a hug. Most of them were in tears and left with a newfound respect for her. For the first time in her life, Bay Bay felt validated. My goal was to teach students not to make fun of people, but also more importantly, never to judge anyone because you don't know what someone has gone through until you have walked in their shoes.

I am sure that when Bay Bay was in the prime of her youth, her goal was not to be a drug addict… but life happened. I tell my students to be careful whom you talk about because one day it could be you. She never again had an issue with the students; in fact, they came to her defense if they saw her being harassed on the street. It's been years since I've left ACE Tech Charter, however, I make it my mission to drive back to the neighborhood to check on Bay Bay. I let her know that I love her and pray for God's protection over her life. I see God in her. Showing love to Bay Bay was nothing new to me. My mother taught me as a young child about the value of humanity. She would invite homeless people to the house to have dinner with us. I thought she was crazy because we barely had enough food to feed ourselves; however, she had a talent for stretching the little we had so that everyone got enough.

My mother was a true humanitarian. I'm thankful to her for instilling in me the mantra of, "Service before self." My mother also had a knack for making people feel special. She could start up a conversation with a complete stranger and you would think that they had known each other for years. The older I get, the more I find myself to be just like her.

ACE Tech Charter High School was located in an area that was heavily influenced by members of the Gangster Disciples (GD's). At this time, we didn't know who the leaders were, but we would soon find out. One afternoon, my students fought a young man who was a GD. This ignited a fight that involved the GD's and students at ACE Tech that would reach epic proportions. The GD's gathered their troops and as students were being released to go home, they started fighting. Between ACE Tech students and the GD's, the fray involved well over 100 people. It was out of control. They were fighting in the street and on sidewalks. Cars had to maneuver around them. It was a spectacular and awful scene. I had to lock students inside the gym to prevent them from taking part in the fight. Because it had progressed to blocks away by the Red Line bus terminal, I rushed there to get my students out of harm's way. The police arrived, but they refused to exit their cars until more help arrived. I was left to handle the situation alone for a few moments. When the cops saturated the scene everyone ran, but returned soon thereafter to start fighting once again. I was outdone. The cops returned and literally chased the instigators down, then placing them under arrest. They put them in the paddy wagon and took them to jail. I knew there would be major backlash to this event, so I prepared myself mentally for what was to follow the next day.

Principal Michael McGrone Sr.

I was in my office when a parent notified me that a large group of Gangster Disciples (GD's) were gathering at KFC and were on their way to the school to retaliate. At that moment, I had a choice to call the police, or confront the issue directly. I chose to face it head-on.

I decided to walk to KFC to meet with the gang members. Mr. Anibal, my assistant, started to walk with me. I told him that I was going alone and that I would be okay, and he thought I was crazy. Mr. Anibal looked like a police officer, and I didn't want them to feel threatened or intimidated. I said a small prayer and headed to KFC. When I got near the restaurant, they all met me outside. I identified myself as the Dean of Students at ACE Tech Charter School. There were about 30 of them. The leader of the gang, named Aaron, approached me and explained that he was upset that members of his crew had been jumped by the guys at ACE Tech Charter. He said that they had jumped the wrong crew this time, and that he was going to show them "who was boss." Aaron had no idea how this chance encounter would change the trajectory of his life. I told him I was here to make peace. I ask the group if they would be willing to walk back to the school with me to resolve the issue. To my surprise, but without hesitation, they obliged. As we walked toward the school, the police pulled up and ask if everything was okay. I assured the police officer that everything was under control. Some of the young men began to panic, and suspected it was a set-up, but I assured them that it was not. I was confident in my ability to create a peaceful and reconcilable situation.

Upon entering the building, one of the security guards noticed the gang moving in behind me. He immediately fled to the main office, and instructed the secretary to call out, "CODE RED!!!

CODE RED!!!" on the intercom. All of the teachers rushed inside their classrooms and locked their doors. As I moved through the school, I couldn't hear a pin drop, but I noticed teachers and students looking outside of their locked classroom doors. Some were frightened, while others were fascinated by this large gang walking through the school in the middle of the day. They either thought I was courageous or just outright crazy!

We made our way upstairs to Room 209 – the detention room. After settling the gang members in, I invited the student leaders at ACE Tech, and anyone else who may have been involved in the incident, to join us. By the time everyone arrived, there was instant tension. The air was so thick you could cut it with a knife. It was clear from the body language in the room that the GD's had their minds on one thing, and one thing only: revenge.

I opened by asking, "Can anyone in this room tell me why we're fighting one another?" No one could. One of my students was staring down one of the young men on the opposing side and the young man responded saying, "See, it's niggas like that who get people killed."

You could feel the room becoming more unsettled by the minute. I got that student out of the room as quickly as I could before the situation irrupted. Right before the room was about to reach a climax, Rodney walked in. At that very moment, Rodney screamed out, "Aaron?!" Aaron from the opposing side said, "Rodney"?!

They both rushed to one another and exchanged a long hug. They hadn't seen each other in over a decade. They both were wards of the state because of their parents' struggle with drug addiction. At this moment, both the students and the gang were left in a state of confusion. Rodney had been at ACE Tech going on his fourth year and had no idea that his brother lived just a block away. That single moment completely shifted the tension in the room. I used this awe-inspiring moment to teach the young men about God's love. Through God's divine intervention, two brothers were reunited after being separated for over 10 years.

Rodney and Aaron.

I had both sides exchange words of reconciliation. Later, they gathered together in a circle with their arms intertwined, and Lewis, an ACE Tech Ambassador, led the group in prayer. It was an awesome sight to see the young men come together in unity. I invited the guys on 55th to come back after school to partake in a game of basketball with my students. I created a challenge that the losing team would be responsible for buying chicken for everyone. Later that night, the group came back, and played my students in a game of basketball. Though my students won, I made them treat the young men to a meal. I thought it was the right thing to do to solidify our relationship with them by showing respect and humility and extending a proverbial olive branch. From that day on, my students and the young men were able to peacefully collaborate and break bread with one another. They did not see each other as bitter enemies, but instead as brothers.

The next day, I was called into the Executive Director's office and was written up for violating the school's safety code. I was scolded for not informing the staff or administration of my plans to bring a gang into the school, and how that incident could've been catastrophic. However, I knew that if I had told the administration what my plans were, they would have never agreed to them. I argued that those young men were not a threat to our community, but rather, they were an asset. We couldn't shield our kids from the culture and environment that they lived in; in fact, our students were simply a reflection of the conditions outside of the school. Needless to say, the school leadership was not having it. To them, I was insubordinate, unprofessional, and

Aaron-BA from Alabama A&M

lacked respect for authority. In so few words, I was told that my time there was limited, and that I should start searching for other employment, just to be on the safe side. The whole incident was a blessing in disguise. Rodney would be reunited with his brother Aaron after being separated for 10 years. Aaron, the leader of the GD's, would leave the street life altogether and graduate from high school. He pursued his dreams by obtaining a Bachelor's Degree from Alabama A&M University. Rodney would defy incredible odds as well, graduating from Morehouse College with his undergraduate degree, from Yale University with two Master's Degrees, and from Harvard University with a Master's Degree in Education. He accomplished all of this in under 10 years. It is a remarkable story, one that I will never forget.

Rodney and I after receiving his BA Degree at Morehouse College
Rodney and I after receiving his Masters Degree from Harvard University.
Me with Rodney after receiving his Masters Degree from Yale University

I became good friends with members of the Gangster Disciples. Though they were gang members, I saw them as aspiring young men who were searching for guidance. They needed someone to lead them in the right direction. Once a month, I would take them out to eat and we laughed and joked. We had a good time and I built a trusting relationship with them. I also met with them for hours on the weekends to get a feel for what was going on in

Members of the Gangster Disciple Nation. Aaron in the center

the streets. Their insight helped keep my students safe. ACE Tech Charter High School was located in an area where shootings and gang wars occurred often. They helped me understand what it was like growing up in Englewood, which is still considered one of the most dangerous communities in Chicago. They never traveled alone, fearing that rival gang members would attack them. They wanted to be prepared at all times. They lived in an area where you had to know where you were going; being unsure or unaware could cost you your life. To keep them off the streets, I allowed them to use our gym. I also let them use the computers to search for jobs, and I taught them how to construct a resume. Throughout the relationship I established with them, my goal was to get them to think more forwardly and to understand that there's more to life than mischievous behavior and hanging out in the streets.

I would only spend one year at ACE Tech, though most of the residents thought I had been there for years. I saw myself as not only belonging to the school, but a servant to the community, as well. At times, I would work seven days a week, doing whatever I could to support them. My conviction to help can be traced back to my childhood, watching my mother serve people who were less fortunate than us. She was always kind to people, despite her own feelings of inadequacies. I would inherit her motivation for selfless acts. Since my departure, the gang has not had any conflicts with the students. I know this because when I return each year, I have conversations with them about what's going on in the neighborhood. They say that out of respect for me, they have avoided getting into any conflicts with the students. Many of the young men have since left the neighborhood and have gone on with their lives. For those who have remained, it's been tough for them. They have lost many of their friends to gun violence, many of whom I knew personally. I always leave by telling them that I love them and to make good choices. I try my best to hook them up with jobs to get them off the streets.

I was a revolutionary educator with a renegade attitude. In my mind, I was on a mission to change the world, starting with the streets of Chicago. I didn't mind that my practices were found to be risky and edgy. I felt that I was doing the right thing because God was guiding my steps.

My deep conviction to this work would take a devastating toll on my family and marriage, and that sacrifice was a hard pill to swallow. My intense dedication meant time away from my wife and children. Most days I would wake up at 6 A.M., and by the time I returned home, everyone would be asleep. On the weekends, I would invite students over to have critical discussions about life. I also wanted them to know the man I was outside of my role as the Dean. I felt compelled to give back because of the promise I had made to God when I was at my lowest. I was blessed beyond measure and my way of repaying God was serving children to the best of my ability. I would come home, eager to talk to Eileen about my experiences at work; however, she refused to hear about them. Her focus was on raising our own children. Ironically, I had stepped outside the marriage thinking it would solve my dilemma, but it would come back to haunt me in a very devastating way. I didn't know how to express what I needed from her and I put my needs above hers. I was looking for a listening ear as a means to cope with the trauma I was experiencing every day.

In time, I would rely on my students to circumvent my thoughts and opinions about these atrocities. I would use these experiences as teachable moments for my students. Having no one to talk to about these experiences drove me deeper into my work with youth, because they were the ones who lived these experiences every day, so quite naturally, they became my outlet. Working with youth became my source of refuge. For better or worse, my conviction to my work became my second marriage. Ultimately, this dichotomy of divesting my time and energy from my family and relationship and investing it all into my students and relationships within the community, led to the dissolution of my marriage.

Going through a divorce was the hardest thing I had ever experienced. I was depressed, angry, confused, retaliatory, and vindictive. My physical and mental health levels were declining. My blood pressure was 220/170. I was on the verge of having a stroke. I was also bleeding out of every orifice of my body. I was on my deathbed.

I became the worst boss you could ever imagine. I took my personal problems out on innocent people. I blamed my ex-wife for the separation at the time, never taking ownership for

Principal Michael McGrone Sr.

Michael Jr., me holding Anaiah and Jeremiah.

what I had done to dissolve the marriage. What I didn't realize though, was that she had "divorced" me years earlier. She learned to live without me. While I was out trying to save the world, I didn't prioritize my marriage, and it took a toll on her. I took her for granted and I didn't realize it until it was too late. The day I moved out of the house, I was an emotional wreck. I was leaving three small children whom I desperately loved. I felt like a total failure and thought that they wouldn't love me anymore. I cried for days. Over time, I began to pray and ask God for forgiveness. I didn't know where to go or whom to turn to. My family provided me with temporary relief, and the few friends that I had told, shared with me what I wanted to hear as opposed to what I needed to hear. Staying on my own gave me time to reflect, and to look deep inside myself. I didn't realize how neglectful I was. I would be physically home, but always emotionally estranged. I allowed going to college and pursuing my career to consume me. After much prayer, I heard God say as plain as day, "Be still." It was at that very moment that I began to gain some wisdom and understanding. Eileen was angry with me and would call me names, but I never would respond with anger. I knew she was hurting too, and I didn't want to exploit or worsen the situation.

When the time came for us to finalize the divorce, I decided that we would go together. The courtroom was packed, filled with angry couples and they all sat apart. You didn't know who was getting a divorce until their names were called to approach the bench, and I didn't want that for us. I wanted to be mature about the situation. We heard all the horrible stories of men not paying child support and women scorned. It was terrible! Eileen leaned over to me and whispered, "Thank you for not treating me like that." I replied, "Never – you're the mother of my children."

When the judge called our names, I was incredibly nervous. My knees buckled but I kept it cool. I did all the paperwork myself, and Eileen and I already had discussed the terms. The judge essentially asked if we both agreed to the terms and conditions of the divorce decree, and we both replied, "Yes." I gave her the house and everything in it; we agreed that the state wouldn't have to deduct money from my check to pay child support, but that I would do it on my own. I could also see my children whenever I wanted. It wasn't difficult, because during the separation we were already fulfilling our obligations. We also didn't want our children to suffer because of our own selfishness. When it was time for us to sign on the dotted line to finalize the divorce, for a brief moment, I was overwhelmed with emotion and began to tear up, but somehow I got through it. It was officially over. Going through a divorce taught me a lot about myself.

I took the focus off of her and began to study where I went wrong. It humbled me. I'm more expressive and allow myself to be vulnerable. Because of the pain I caused in my marriage, I wanted to be there for her and the kids even more. She and I are good friends, and the relationship we have with our children is great. I told her to *never* worry about me paying child support, even if it meant that I had to go without. My obligation was to her and my kids. I wanted her to feel secure. She would always thank me for sending her child support payments, to which I would tell her, "You don't thank a man for doing what he's supposed to do."

I'm very careful as to how I treat my ex-wife, knowing that my children are vigilantly watching. We laugh often, and from time to time, I give her a hug for being such a great mother. I want my kids to know that despite it all, I admire their mother for the sacrifices she made. I make sure that for every holiday and birthday, the kids celebrate *her*. We allow our children to discuss their feelings to make sure they feel whole. In many ways, my divorce marked the end of the old Michael McGrone Sr., and the beginning of the new me.

My divorce almost cost me my life. I am grateful that God preserved me and allowed me to see that there is life after divorce. My goal for this next journey is to truly allow God to guide my steps. Life is short, and I choose to be happy.

Chapter 11

THE ROAD AHEAD

I consider myself to be in the midst of self-evolution. Through God's grace, I've been able to achieve many of my lifelong goals. I never miss an opportunity to reflect on the fact that I graduated from high school with only a 1.2 GPA. Being constantly told by my mother that I was marginal at best became a self-debilitating prophecy. I became good at failing. Nonetheless, through my past struggles with homelessness, abuse and depression, I have excelled in ways that I couldn't have ever imagined. I worked at Seton Academy Catholic School, located in South Holland, Illinois as the Dean of Students. Just as when I worked at numerous other schools previously, the policies were rarely enforced so I came in strong. I did a lot of creative planning there to keep students in school. Students who came late to school were required to pick up trash near the expressway and clean up in and around the school, and of course they despised it. Many of the individuals in detention were exceptional athletes on the basketball team, but I didn't care. I wanted the student body to understand that everyone is treated the same in the matter of consequences.

However, because some of the basketball players had a sense of entitlement, I was even tougher on them. Two popular basketball players got into a physical altercation. The fight was bad, and they both were seriously injured. I also found out that another student had instigated the fight. Rather than suspend them, I came up with an innovative idea to keep them in school. I had each of them dress in orange jumpsuits. They had to stand directly behind each other. I blindfolded two of them while the one in front marched them around the school. The goal was to get them to trust each other as they took turns. I marched them to exhaustion. The only time they sat down was to eat lunch. When I went to my office to finish work, I still required them to march in place. Though they were tired, they were appreciative that they didn't get suspended. After the ordeal, they learned a great deal from one another. They didn't have any other problems for the remainder of the year.

Restoring discipline was fairly simple for me. However, the challenge for me was the principal who rarely showed up for work, which meant that the bulk of the responsibility fell on me. It was alleged that she was having a relationship with one of the coaching staff members on the basketball team. I had serious issues with this because it impacted the culture and climate of the school, as everyone was gossiping about it and was distracted by it. I saw her and the coach together and my instinct told me something was not right. The Chicago Arch Diocese would end up investigating the matter. The Principal would eventually resign amidst the controversy, and the brunt of the responsibility for taking care of the student fell upon me.

The boys' basketball team was really good that year and won the school's first state title in any sport. All of the news outlets and fans waited anxiously at the school as we received a police escort. As we exited the bus, people were clapping and cheering on the team. Everyone was passing around the first-place state championship trophy as pictures were being taken. It was a joyous occasion. The following week, the coaching staff and the principal were fitted with championship rings, and though I was an administrator and was considered Seton's number one super fan, I never received a ring. I was still considered an outsider.

I only worked at Seton Academy for one year and just as I had with all of the other schools, the turnaround rate was significant. Attendance increased up to 95%, tardies decreased by 80% and there was a significant decline in suspensions by 85%. College acceptance rates rose to 95%. The students and staff made working there fun. It prepared me for my next big task at Bishop Noll Institute.

At Bishop Noll Institute (a Catholic School in Hammond, Indiana) I would become the first African American Assistant Principal in the school's 88-year history. It was historic because I was neither Catholic nor did I graduate from Bishop Noll, and they typically hired from within the ranks. Being the first African American staff member, however, did not come without criticism. A group of parents banded together and wrote letters to the Indiana Board of Education, challenging my credentials. They said that I was not qualified, though there were numerous administrators throughout Indiana who did not have said "credentials." They put pressure on the Principal, so she said I would have to change my title on the website. I was furious because I thought that she didn't defend me in the way she should have. I knew I was being singled out solely because of the color of my skin. In another incident, someone created a fake Facebook account using my name and likeness referring to me as an "ape," "coon" and "monkey."

Students were responding to those posts using derogatory language. I did not know that this Facebook account existed until I was notified by the technology teacher. I was angry because this was the first time that something like this happened to me. I felt as if I was living in the Jim Crow era. I met with the Principal and Superintendent, and even involved the police because it was considered a hate crime. Matters would get more complicated when a parent approached me and stated that she did not want me meeting with her daughter alone. I responded, telling her that if her daughter had an issue that I would meet with her alone; however, I would certainly contact her to inform her what the issue was. To resolve the certification complaint, I was able to get a provisional license because I was currently attending Governors State University to get my administrative degree. However, this left me angry and upset because I was not being treated equal to everyone else. Everywhere I went, I was stared at and even questioned whether I was the Assistant Principal of Bishop Noll Institute (BNI). To combat this issue, the athletic director, Ed, bought me a letterman jacket with my name on it: "Mike McGrone Sr., Assistant Principal."

His hopes were that people would stop questioning me seeing that I wore a legitimate BNI Jacket. I wore this jacket at every event I attended to minimize the questioning. I was grateful. Ed was an older white gentleman who had worked at BNI for over 35 years in various capacities. He was a jewel. He arrived to work before anyone, cleaning up and making sure everything was in order. He loved working with children and did whatever he could to make sure they had a great experience at Bishop Noll. He and I are still good friends to this day; I lovingly refer to him as "my brother from another mother." He also is a former resident of Gary. Though I would go on to experience other forms of racism, I didn't allow this to distract me. Most of the families and staff treated me with the utmost respect and the students were exceptional.

Like most places I've worked, I hit the ground running. My first focus was on restoring discipline. In collaboration with the students, faculty, and staff, we revised the student handbook to make it relevant to the times. One example is I allowed students to use their cell phones, but only during designated times. They loved it because they could communicate with their friends and parents during school hours. It drastically cut down on the number of referrals that were written. To hold students accountable for their behavior, I put a stop to detention being served on designated days. For example, if a student committed an infraction on a Monday, they had to serve detention on the same day. My goal was to minimize the frequency of behavior problems. This angered some of the parents and students, but I was not intimidated. I stayed focused and the impact was felt immediately. The results were dramatic. There was a significant reduction in suspensions and reportable incidents.

Students understood that I meant business. I always served detention alongside the students, which was after school. When students found out that I was the one managing detentions, they did whatever they could to avoid getting in trouble. We cleaned walls, mopped floors, and cleaned the trophy cases that hadn't been cleaned in years. Once we finished cleaning, I would take them to my office and talk to them about life. What I discovered was that most of them were dealing with significant challenges in their life and were acting out. As they shared their stories, others began to share too, and they discovered they were not alone. It became a spiritual experience, and though many of the students could go home, they wanted to stay to talk through their problems. I stayed with them as long as they wanted to talk. This happened often. The goal was not to punish them, but to use that time as an opportunity to teach them. I wanted students to know that although I was tough, I cared about them. The students slowly began to understand that I was there to serve them and they started to open up to me.

I was Bishop Noll Institute's number one super fan. My final year at BNI, the basketball team went undefeated during the regular season, 26-0. Every game we played, we managed to win. It was an exciting time! I wrote several chants that I practiced with the students, and boy did they take it to the next level! I had the students repeat after me, "Well this is Bishop... Yeah... The mighty Bishop... Yeah...We gonna win this game tonight... alright, alright." The whole crowd joined in. Students came to the games dressed as cartoon characters, ketchup bottles, even biblical characters! It was quite a sight. The cheer section had more than half of the student body in attendance and they got the crowd pumped. I had never seen anything like it before. It was Indiana basketball at its finest. They were truly "The 6th Man."

The basketball team made it all the way to the state finals. We were set to play Park Tudor High School for the Class 2A championship. The students were dressed and ready to cheer on their team. The Park Tudor fans were ready as well, but they would be no match for Bishop Noll's cheer section. They cheer-challenged us, but we shut them down. There was no way we were going to let them out-cheer us. I led the cheer block and we rocked the arena. The game was intense. The lead changed numerous times. Park Tudor was up by 1 point with 8 seconds left on the clock, and we had the ball. It was the most nervous I had been during the entire season. In the closing seconds, Ronnie dribbled the ball to the top of the key. As time was ticking down, 5… 4… 3… 2… 1, he went up to make the jump shot he had made a thousand times right before the buzzer went off. It all seemed to happen in slow motion. The ball spun around the rim several times, but came out. It was a devastating loss. The students were crushed and many began crying. I had to console them. I reminded them it was their support that helped the basketball team make it this far.

To my surprise, the Governor of Indiana approached me and asked who I was. I told him I was the Assistant Principal, and he was surprised. He said that he had never seen an administrator interact with the students the way I did. I told him I was Bishop Noll's number one super fan. I also told him that the students loved their school and that they had great traditions. I wanted to make sure we continued with those traditions. Though it was a tough loss, I was proud of the students because they made coming to the games so exciting. I was grateful to be part of such a historical season. A picture of me with the players and coaches is placed in the gym of that historic day. When it was all said and done, I was honored to have been accepted into Bishop Noll's family. I've been invited back on several occasions to speak at graduation. I recited chants and remarkably, the students remembered them after all these years. They were hyped, as usual. I was happy to see that they were keeping the traditions alive. It felt like the old days.

During my tenure at BNI, I was able to complete my Master's Degree in Educational Leadership. The program was *intense*. Several of my classmates would end up quitting within the first several weeks. At that time, my marriage was failing and I was having a difficult time focusing. This began to impact my grades. Fortunately, my professors worked with me and I was able to make up missed class assignments.

My final semester at Governors State, my good friend Coach Gray allowed me to study at his house due to the stress I was dealing with at home. I had first met Coach Gray in 2001. He and I became good friends because of our shared passion for working with children. His life revolved around building up young men. In 2005, he got a Head Football Coaching position at Marshall High School, located on the West Side of Chicago in a tough neighborhood (Jackson and Kedzie). He was looking for coaches

Marshall Coaching Staff

to hire that not only understood the game but could also identify with the players. He recruited me and several other exceptional coaches. They were experts at their craft. My role, however, would be much more unique than that of a traditional coach. I would serve as the "Spiritual Advisor." The players on the team were wounded and played the game angrily. I understood what they were going through because I had played football with the same aggression. On this particular day, Coach Gray asked if I could meet with the team to draw them closer together. As I shared my story with them, they began to open up. I wanted them to know that they did not have to suffer in silence anymore. One by one, they began to share their stories.

One player talked about being shot, another talked about being homeless, another talked about being a young father and selling drugs to support his family. These were *high school* students. The emotions in the room were quite intense, and it would be the first time that many of the players were able to release pent-up anger. There was not a dry eye left in the room. Coach Gray rushed into the room, not knowing what was going on, and I explained to him this was the result of players not being heard and suffering alone. I would end up having sessions like this frequently before games to make sure they were mentally prepared. We became a close family.

However, this one particular student struck me as being arrogant. His name was "Chubb." He recently transferred in from another school. The first day I met him he had his shirt off. I said, "who are you?" He replied, "My name is Chubb and I'm the best player out here." I told him you have a lot to prove before you can open your mouth to say something like that. He then told me to watch him. As practice went along, I would realize just how good he was. He was a ferocious hitter and could run the ball like I've never seen from a high school athlete. He also had good football instincts. I didn't tell him how good he really was feeling it would only inflate his ego, but he was the best athlete I have ever seen. Chubb had serious anger problems. One incident he broke Coach Gray's windows out his car and got into several altercations with the coaching staff. Coach Gray and I went to talk with his mother and upon surveying the home we noticed that part of the roof was missing and was covered in plastic. How he lived reminded me of my own experiences. His mother didn't know what to do with him and his father did not play an active role in his life. Meeting with his Mom gave us more insight as to what angered him. He was never given a chance and football was his outlet. He excelled at football, and was a leader. It helped with his self-esteem and he thrived. I learned how to be patient with him. Knowing what he was going through, Coach Gray allowed him to spend the night at his house and took care of him. We had subsequent meetings like this with other players who were going through tough times. For a player who received special education services, I served as their advocate and made sure they were being treated fairly. I made sure the school officials did their job.

We didn't have a practice facility, so we had to walk over to Huron Park, a block away from the school. The park was filled with homeless people. They had sleeping bags and tents set up alongside the field where we practiced; drug dealers also saturated the park. Before we could start practice, Coach Gray would line the entire team up across the field to pick up broken glass and discard drug needles. There were so many distractions that one of our main goals was to keep the guys focused. Coach Gray believed in conditioning. He would run the players to exhaustion. It was not usual for him to run them up and down the field for as long as 30 to 40 minutes straight. I was tired of watching them. I remember jokingly telling him that I was going to report him to the Department of Children and Family Services (DCFS) for child abuse. However, his tactics would prove successful as the season progressed. There were times that our opponent was tired and we were just getting warmed up. They would come to the sideline and tell Coach Gray, "They tired... Run the ball behind me." The games we were behind, they found a way to win. They never held their head low; they banded together as brothers and got the job done. In many games, we won in spectacular fashion in the closing seconds.

To inspire the young men, I taught them a poem called "See It Through" by Edgar Guest. I required them to recite it after each game, win or loss. It became our tradition.

Coach Gray receiving the runner up Chicago City Championship trophy.

In Coach Grey's first year as the Head Coach, we went 10-0. Unfortunately, we lost to King High School in the Chicago Conference City Championship game. I was so proud of our players though. They defied incredible odds. They never made excuses, and didn't cheat during the game. They worked hard. What impressed me even more with Coach Gray is that he used football as a metaphor for life to teach the young men about manhood. The coaching staff is still connected with many of the players, and when time permits we still get together to reminisce about that magical season. Many of the players are now fathers and successful in their own right.

Coach Gray's support during one of the most difficult times in my life was invaluable. I would go on to graduate from Governors State University with a 3.8 GPA. He, along with my brother, Kenyon, attended my graduation ceremony. Coach Gray threw me the biggest graduation party at his home, and didn't ask me for a dime. I was so grateful for his generosity. My family, as well as my friends, came to celebrate with me. I would go on to successfully to pass the Illinois Type 75 State Exam on the first attempt to become a certified school administrator. It was truly a remarkable journey.

After graduating from Governors State, my professor asked me if I were ever offered a principal's position, would I take it? I told him I didn't think I was ready; he advised not to be surprised if it happened. I didn't know how prophetic his words would prove to be in just a few days.

I interviewed and accepted a position at a charter school in the City of Chicago, paying a six-figure salary as an Associate Principal and set to begin in July 2011. In the coming weeks, I discovered that Harvey School District 152 was looking to hire an Assistant Principal for one of their elementary schools, so I applied for it as well. I didn't think too much of it because I already had a job lined up. To my surprise, I was called in for an interview. I interviewed at the District Office among teachers, the Union representative, district office staff and Superintendent Kellogg. They were so impressed with the interview that they asked if I would consider taking the Principal's position at Lowell-Longfellow Elementary

School. I was shocked!

They needed a response that very day. I called my mentor to get his advice. He recommended that I accept the role because it would put me in a position to learn how to run a building and what it takes to be an instructional leader. I prayed about the situation and ended up accepting the offer. I was grateful that they had faith in me that I was the right person for the job. I called the charter school and told them I had another job offer. I got to work right away. I discovered quickly that Lowell-Longfellow Elementary School was located in one of the most dangerous areas in Harvey, Illinois. Drug addicts roamed the streets, drug dealers were rampant, gangs ruled the neighborhood and in some neighborhoods, there were more abandoned homes than actual homes. As you can imagine, it was a high crime area. When I entered the main entrance, I discovered it was riddled with bullet holes. I was comfortable working in communities like this because it reminded me so much of the neighborhood I grew up in. My goal was to create partnerships with the people in the neighborhood where they didn't see me as an outsider, but instead understood that I was there to serve them.

Lowell Project clean the community

I was able to use the education model that I most believed in since I got started in education, transforming the school culture and climate from the outside in. It was clear to me that we would not be able to move the school in a positive direction unless we addressed the social and systemic elements that impacted the local children and families. Before I set foot in the building, I walked door-to-door, introducing myself to the neighbors. I wanted to gain insight on some of the challenges that were in the community and how I could best serve them. Their input was invaluable because I was able to educate the staff on the social and systemic elements that impacted how the students learned and the needs of the community. One of the primary concerns

Lowell school project clean the community

they expressed was how filthy their community was and the number of abandoned homes within a three-block radius – thirty-two, to be exact. To address the trash issue in the community, I came up with a new project: "Clean Harvey, One Block at a Time." Every weekend, I, along with staff, students, and residents, walked throughout the neighborhood, picking up trash. I also took my children along with me to teach them about valuing and respecting humanity and nature. It was a sight to see – over fifty participants walking the streets block-by-block, picking up trash. Our first weekend,

Lowell School collect 32 bag of trash in 3 blocks

Lowell students stand beside garbage can they placed throughput the community

we collected over thirty-two bags of trash, including over one hundred liquor bottles in three blocks. It was a proud moment for everyone because we were taking charge of the community. We also painted the garbage cans red and white, with "Lowell School" on them, and placed them throughout the community. Residents from the community would prepare meals for the participants to eat; I received help from District 152, as well. This went on throughout my tenure at Lowell School. The abandoned buildings were a major concern because they were a safety hazard and haven for drug addicts. Students wrote letters to the mayor to have these structures demolished. Within weeks, they saw homes being torn down that had been eyesores for years. They felt proud of their accomplishment. I didn't want them to feel bad about their neighborhood, so many times we had class right there on the street to discuss ways they could improve the conditions. The ideas they came up with were truly remarkable. I then told them every time they walked past an abandoned building to say to themselves, "I'm the one," which meant one

Principal Michael McGrone Sr.

Having class with Students in their neighborhood

day they would make their community better. One day, one of my favorite students in the second grade came rushing into my office out of breath. She exclaimed with excitement in her voice, "Mr. McGrone, guess what? I saw an abandoned building and guess what I said? I'm the one... I'm the one that's going to make my community better." She got it! She was a wonderful soul. She handed me a flower on the last day of school that she had plucked from a neighbor's yard. I told her that I loved her and to

Me posing with the student who's going to make her community better

never lose focus. I know she is going to do great things in her life. The seed had been planted.

Walking with staff in the community   *Walking with staff through the community*

To educate staff on the social systemic dysfunction that impacted students in the community, I scheduled meetings on the outside where we would literally meet in front of the abandoned buildings. Because most of the staff members did not live in the community, I wanted to expose them to what the students were dealing with every day. The ultimate goal was for them to utilize the experiences of the students to drive instruction and motivate them to become active participants in the learning process.

As I mentioned earlier, Lowell School was located in one of the deadliest parts of Harvey. I spent numerous summers getting to know the neighbors and talking to my students. Many of the residents had my personal cell phone number and would contact me if anything happened in the community that impacted my students. I wanted to engross myself in the community to have a better understanding as to what the students' experiences were, but more importantly, my goal was to use those experiences to help motivate them to learn using real-life experiences. What I learned in particular with children who live in high poverty areas is that they learn best when they see it as part of their survival. I wanted the learning process to be meaningful for them and for them to not see it as a waste of time. I wanted them to know that it was a life-or-death decision.

The four years I served as principal at Lowell School, a neighbor was killed by the police attempting to rob a grocery store, one of my student's parents was murdered, three young men who I developed a close relationship in the community were killed by gun violence, a student's home was raided by a SWAT team alleging that her parents were dealing drugs, several students' homes burned down (I had to provide temporary shelter for one of the families at Lowell School, and I contacted the Red Cross and took them shopping for toiletries and clothes because they had lost everything) and a drug addict died in an abandoned home nearby of an apparent overdose.

All of these incidents happened within a three-block radius of where my students lived. My students came to school traumatized or desensitized, and I had to do something about it. Having this information was invaluable. I used it to assist teachers in finding strategic ways to help students cope with the trauma they were being exposed to on a daily basis. I wanted them to provide activities that allowed students to discuss incidents they were dealing with in the community and that would allow them to debrief. As the principal, my goal was to create a culture where the students felt safe and loved. It was also important to me that every student got a hot breakfast, and I was blessed to have staff members who came to work early to make sure they got just that.

I knew it would be very difficult to raise academic achievement levels without first dealing with the students' trauma. Rarely did

The Twists & Turns of Possibility

Students completing homework during lunch-- Me helping student with homework

students receive counseling about what they witnessed or were victims of. Challenges were so great in the homes of students that homework assignments were rarely completed. Thus, I required them to eat for the first ten minutes of the lunch period; the final twenty minutes I required them to complete homework assignments, study and make up missed class assignments. I did not care about them being upset. I was willing to do whatever it took for them to be successful. Eventually, the students got used to it. Students worked both independently and in groups. The teachers also used their prep time to tutor students. They did not ask to be compensated. They sacrificed their time and energy to ensure that the students were successful. It was a true team effort.

The new Common Core state standardized test would be the greatest challenge for the teachers and students. The teachers did their best to prepare students for the rigor; however, they were still concerned because part of their evaluation was based on student achievement from a new state standardized test. Even more frustrating, the teachers could no longer have information

Principal Michael McGrone Sr.

Student using picture of mom to motivate her for test

displayed on their walls for students to refer to as they took the test. To motivate students, I allowed them to bring pictures of beloved family members that would inspire them to do their best. They placed the pictures next to them as they prepared to take the computer-based test. I went around to each student, inquiring who the person was in the picture. I wanted them to give me a historical perspective of their life, but more particularly, explain what the person meant to them. I would use this to inspire them. It was emotional because most of their relatives in the pictures were deceased. The students had pictures of their mothers, fathers, grandmothers, aunts, uncle, sisters, brothers and so on. I told them that when they felt like giving up, to refer to the picture for motivation. It was inspirational watching them become so focused. That year, they made significant gains in reading and math. The teachers did an outstanding job working with the students. With the challenges they were presented with, they never made excuses. They held them to a higher standard and expected them to do their best.

There were a number of young men in the community with felony convictions. It was a huge problem, because many of them were simply *existing*. I knew how that felt because of my own experience of feeling hopeless. Many of them coped with the inability to find work because of their drug and alcohol use. To combat this problem, I arranged to have expungement summits on the weekends. I consulted with attorneys from the local court, Markham Court House, to educate the young men on how to clear their records. Many of them had been forced into a life of crime because they had a difficult time finding employment due to their prior convictions. These young men wanted more for themselves, and I felt compelled to help them succeed.

To support families who didn't have food, I started a food pantry at Lowell School. Mrs. Rogers, the Board President of Harvey School District 152 at the time, played a critical role. With her influence, she made sure I had everything I needed to provide food for the families. When they came to pick up baskets of food, the District 152 food service also provided a hot meal. It was a team effort, and my staff was there to serve them too. We also gave away clothes, and for parents who needed social and emotional support, we met once a month for round table discussions. The sessions

Lowell School Social Emotional Group   Lowell School Community Meeting

were intense. I recall one mother who said she was gang raped by several men while waiting for a train. She said that one of the men had AIDS, which she contracted. After the ordeal, she found out that she was pregnant. Remarkably, she decided to keep the baby; however, she explains every so often that she hates looking at the child because the child reminds her of the incident that happened. It was the most traumatic testimony I've ever heard, and we all cried with her. Stories such as hers inspire me even more to have social and emotional roundtable discussions to help parents find ways to cope when tragedy happens. For many of them, it would be the first time they shared their darkest pain. They were able to express themselves in an authentic way without being judged, and it was truly a transformative experience. Having infrastructure like this allowed me to pay homage to my mother who never got the support she desperately needed. She suffered from mental health issues and felt embarrassed. I never want another mother to suffer as my mother did. I understand that by stabilizing the life of the parent, you can improve on the life of a child and, by default, they will perform better in school. I came up with the slogan: "Better parents make better children."

Over 95% of the students who attended Lowell School lived in complete poverty. One day, one of my favorite students came to my office crying. I had to calm her down. She was in kindergarten. She had the most beautiful black complexion and a smile that could brighten up a room. She referred to me as "Prince McGrone" and I referred to her "Princess." Her family reminded me of my own. She had ten siblings, and they struggled to make ends meet and couldn't afford to buy designer clothes. She told me that students were making fun of her because her clothes were worn and outdated. She said they even made fun of her shoes because they had holes at the bottom. They then told her she was ugly.

As she stood there crying, I told her to look directly into my eyes and repeat after me, "I'm smart and I'm pretty." She said it; however, her voice was trembling from all of the crying. I told her to repeat it again, this time with more confidence. She said, "I'm SMART and I'm PRETTY!"

I told her to never allow other students to break her spirits and that if she needed to cry to come into my office. I explained to her that what makes her "smart and pretty" is her attitude and how kind she was to everyone. Seeing that her shoes were badly worn, I had her remove her shoes and a staff member volunteered to buy her a new pair. I kept her shoes as a reminder of how far I've come because I too had shoes like those and if I could do it, I knew she could as well. I always say, "Struggles prepare you for greatness."

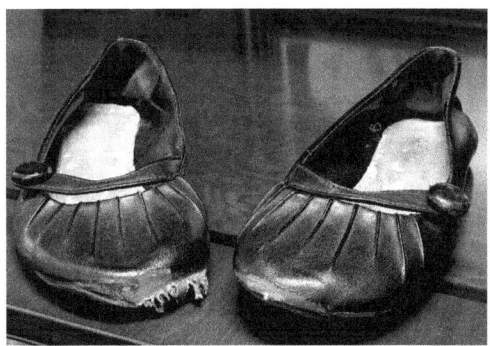

The students worn shoes I keep in my office

She may have started off with worn shoes, but that won't be how the story ends. I'm a living witness. When I do see her again, I want to remind her of just how far she's come ("The journey of a thousand steps start with one"). This incident would lead to the creation of the Lowell School's creed. Because students lacked

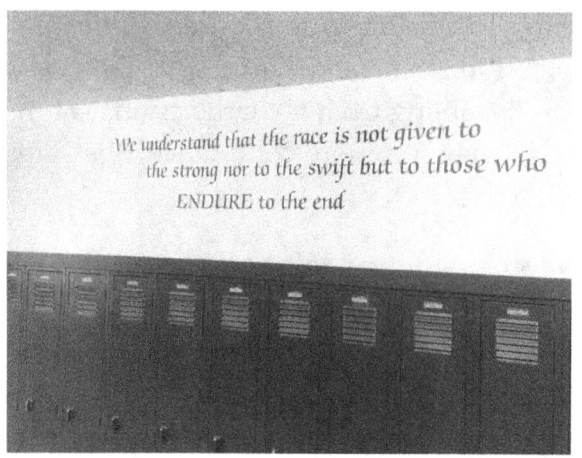

I placed Lowell's school creed throughout the building

respect for each other and school spirit, I got together with the staff and we wrote the school creed. Every morning at 7:30 A.M., we gathered the students in the gym; when the weather was warm, we would meet outside. The students lined up by grade level in a straight line to recite the creed. Each grade was represented. It was exciting to watch, especially when we were outside. Parents were even invited to attend. As the students recited the creed, the residents would peek outside their windows. They were so loud that it echoed throughout the community. The girls concluded their portion of the creed by saying, "I'm smart and I am pretty" and the boys, "I'm smart and I'm a soldier!" They loved it! I wanted them to be proud of their school. I took parts of the school creed and had it placed throughout the building. One segment is mixed with my favorite bible verse: "We understand that the race is not given to the strong nor to the swift but to the ones who endure to the end." It was proudly located near the main entrance.

As I explained earlier, my divorce took a huge toll on me emotionally. I took the pain of my personal life out on my staff. Sometimes I wouldn't speak to them, and my attitude was terrible. My secretary, Mrs. Alexander (may she rest in peace) would always ask me if I was okay, and I would always tell her yes. Her and I were very close and she knew something was wrong, but I never told her the truth. I needed help, and I didn't know how to ask for it. She would try to talk to me about how my behavior was impacting the teachers, and I would just tune her out. The climate was at an all-time low. I became the worst principal ever. Staff meetings were tense, and I led with an iron fist or lashed out. Things would get even worse when I threatened to involve District 152 board members if the teachers didn't comply with demands I was making. They didn't take well to these kinds of threats and would involve their union president, but I didn't care. My weight was dropping, and I was depressed.

It was at this time that Mrs. Alexander confronted me and told me to come clean. I broke down in tears and told her everything. To my surprise, she knew the whole time what I was going through, but never said anything. She hoped I would confide in her, so that she could help me. She helped me understand the serious impact I had on my staff and how ultimately it was negatively affecting the students. I was totally oblivious; I thought I was being a good leader all along.

I prayed and ask God for wisdom as to how I would deal with this situation. I had the weekend to process what I was going to say to my staff. I told Mrs. Alexander to schedule meetings with each teacher individually in my office. I wanted to apologize to each of them personally for making work conditions so miserable. They were apprehensive to meet, understandably; however, I altered the narrative. I told them how sorry I was for my actions and revealed to them parts of my personal life. I explained to them how emotionally wounded I was and that they did not deserve what I put them through. They were shocked at how transparent I was. I saw the effect right before my eyes. I told them from this moment on I would be the principal they'd always wanted.

Principal Michael McGrone Sr.

Lowell School Teachers

The family atmosphere we created translated into student achievement. I spent a lot of time in the classrooms. I learned how talented the teachers really were and the investments they made in the lives of our students. They taught me a valuable lesson: to whom much is given, much is required. I learned that leadership is nothing more than relationships. Your staff has to trust you and know that you have their backs. The challenges we had at Lowell School were insurmountable, but the staff was truly dedicated. They never allowed students to make excuses and pushed them to be the greatest they could be. They worked extra hours on the weekends and even helped clean the community. They never asked for additional pay. I will never forget my experience as the principal of Lowell School. Unfortunately, Lowell school was demolished on August 27, 2018; however, the memories will last a lifetime. My experiences at Lowell School solidified my leadership style as a public servant and transformational leader.

As time would tell, Lowell School would prepare me for my biggest challenge of all. In 2015, I accepted a position as the principal of Rich South High School, in Richton Park, Illinois. Rich

Rich South High School

Township District 227 had been in turmoil for years. I spoke with my mentors, and they discouraged me from taking the position. They said it would destroy my career. The District 227 Board of Education members were fighting amongst themselves, there were issues with the superintendents, and the community was fed up. All of the dysfunction trickled down and had a profound effect on the students and staff in the Rich Schools (South, Central and East). The schools were dangerous, teachers were frustrated, and the climate and culture were at an all-time low. With all of the turmoil going on in the District, it would seem obvious that I would turn down the position.

However, I never ran from a problem during my career; as a matter of fact, the greater the challenge, the more attracted I was to it. I always considered myself to be a "turnaround specialist." As God spoke to me, it became clear that this was my next assignment. The President of the Board had been observing me for years. He saw how progressive I was and knew I had the right temperament and assertiveness to take on the job. He scheduled a meeting with me and several other board members so that they could get a feel for my working style. We talked for hours. They wanted me to know how serious they were about moving the district forward. They also wanted to know specific information as to my plan to change the culture at Rich South High School and raise academic achievement. I had done my research and was prepared for the task. I assured them that I would not let them down; I wanted them to know that I was the man for the job. I had no idea of the extent of the politics that went along with this high-stake position. Numerous articles were written about how ineffective I would be. For example, one article said that I didn't have any high school experience, that I came from a failing school, I didn't know anything about standardized testing and that I was related to one of the Board members, all of which were not true. This fueled me even more to do my very best!

I would be responsible for approximately 1100 students and over 100 staff members. I heard all of the rumors about how bad Rich South was; however, I was not intimidated. I anticipated the challenge. My sister Kim and I walked the entire parameter of school in prayer. My mother and other members of my family gathered at the front entrance and prayed for God to guide my steps. My first time walking the halls of Rich South, I cried, thanking God for his blessings and mercy on my life. I knew my father would be proud of me. I had promised him on December 14th, the day he passed away, that I would make something of myself, and the stage was now set.

Mrs. LaCour, the Associate Principal of Teaching and Learning, was the first administrator I met. She and I were hired at the same time, but I had no idea who she was. I literally met her when she walked passed my office door, and I stopped her to ask her name. She was tough and smart. She had a thorough understanding of her craft, and I was thoroughly impressed. Her and I shared the same teaching philosophy and we made a good team. She was a resident of the community and was familiar with the issues

District 227 had been having for years. She had heard all of the "bad" stories about Rich South, as well. We were committed to turning Rich South around and were confident that we would not fail.

Mr. Gordan was the Associate Principal of Buildings and Grounds. He was the veteran in the group, with over twenty years of experience. He had great insight as to what we were up against. His knowledge would prove invaluable, as we would put our heads together to begin the transformation.

In the following months, we hired Mr. Shrodrof as the Athletic Director. He complemented the group well. He was a hard worker and revolutionized the athletic department.

My administrative team (L to R, Mr. Gordan, Mrs. LaCour, Me, Mr. Schdrof and Mr. Epps

The next year we hired Mr. Epps as the Director of Special Education who was an up-and-coming administrator. The team

Morning meeting with staff.

was in place. What was most impressive about my leadership team is that we had each other's back.

My first goal was to create an environment where students and staff felt safe. My first year, I came in guns blazing. I didn't believe in honeymoon periods. Students quickly figured out that I was not there to play games. I wanted to make clear that students were no longer running the school. *I* was the new sheriff in town. I ruled the school with an iron fist and a velvet glove. My thoughts were that the principal dictated the culture and climate of the school, not the students. Though some of my methods were unorthodox, the results were proven to be effective. My focus was also to repair relationships among staff that had been compromised. To improve communication, each morning I required my administrative team, security, deans, hall monitors and social workers to be in attendance for the morning meeting. We met in a circle in the cafeteria right before I delivered the morning message. We had critical and engaging conversations about student achievement, safety concerns and upcoming activities. Starting the day off on this foot changed the culture and attitude of the building. We trusted

Delivering my morning message to students

each other and got the job done! Once we were done meeting, we went around to check on our students to make sure they were doing well and ready for instruction.

As opposed to making intercom announcements, I preferred talking to my students directly: all 1,100 of them in the cafeteria right before they went to class. I was told it couldn't be done (i.e., they would be too disruptive, they wouldn't focus, they wouldn't listen). I knew my potential and what I was capable of. I'd done it at every school I had worked at. My thoughts were that students will only do what you allow. I was taught to be fearless and there was no way I was going to let students take control. Again, my belief was that the Principal dictated the culture and climate of the building. The students had no idea what was in store for them. I stood on a chair in the cafeteria where everyone could see me. The first couple of days, I had to scream at the top of my lungs to get their attention. I reminded them that I was going to do this every day until they conformed to my expectations. They didn't take me seriously, so I did the same thing every day for a couple of weeks. Soon, they realized that I was not going to stop. Within weeks, students were quiet and paying attention, and I never had to raise my voice. The students now look forward to the morning message (well, some did). However, the key is consistency, holding students accountable and maintaining the conviction in what you are doing. I always thought it was important to gather students in the morning to set the tone for the day. I did it for a couple of reasons: 1) to motivate students, 2) to discuss upcoming activities, and 3) to support students dealing with any personal issues before going to class. Students also made announcements;

Student leading the morning meeting

however, they were not your typical announcements. Students discussed the environment of the school, bullying, domestic violence, depression, suicide and many other serious topics. It was truly remarkable to watch them take charge. In one morning session, a student was reunited with his father after not seeing him for more than ten years. It was remarkably emotional. We had numerous situations like that occur, and entire lives were transformed. Students even used that time to pray together. The goal was for students to take ownership of "their" school. I often asked the students, "Whose school is this?" and they responded in unison, "My school!"

Lunch periods at Rich South were the best! They gave me an opportunity to get to know my students on a personal level. We laughed, joked and had fun. Every Friday I devoted my entire day to my students. My staff knew I was not to be disturbed. We had our very own "DJ Buckwild." He came in every Friday to play the latest rap and R&B cuts. He was also responsible

DJ Buckwild
Rich South 'Turnup" Friday

Principal Michael McGrone Sr.

Me with students on "Turnup" Friday

for a lot of the celebrity guest who volunteered to perform for our students. We had live bands and all. Our 'Turnup" Fridays went viral and school across the country copied what we did. Buckwild and I developed a close relationship. He helped me connect with my students through music. I spared no expense, I had DJ Buckwild order bouncy houses and other games to help us celebrate student achievement, attendance, students keeping the school safe, and so on. I danced with the students and they even taught me the latest dance moves. I enjoyed seeing my students have fun.

Staff would also take part in the festivities. I always believed that music was the great equalizer. DJ Buckwild would play "old school" music for the staff enjoyment as well.

Every Wednesday and twice every month, I mentored a group of young men. We discussed a myriad of topics. I allowed them time to vent, discuss school-related issues, violence in the community, how to solve conflicts, and we even meditated. Sometimes, I allowed them to sleep to calm their souls after having endured

Me mentoring our boys.

a traumatic experience. The sessions were intense. The group consisted of the most challenging students in the school; however, I transformed them into leaders. Once known for being bullies and starting fights, they were now breaking up fights. It awesome seeing students become peacemakers in the community. What I discovered is that these students needed to feel connected to the school. It now became OUR school. It was remarkable to see surveillance footage of students breaking up fights of their own volition before security even arrived on the scene.

Everyday at 6 A.M., I arrived to work to pray and meditate. This time was sacred to me because it was the only time I had to myself before the students arrived at school. It was at that time that God would speak to me in the stillness of the air and give me the wisdom I needed to run the school. Every Monday I allowed members of the male leadership team to take part in my daily ritual. They would walk with me throughout the halls as I was in prayer asking God to guide my steps. I was in tears, grateful for His wisdom and mercy. My students knew not to talk to me during this time. I wanted to teach them the meaning of the mantra, "To whom much is given, much is required." Leadership is about humility, role-modeling your expectations, and being

the change you expect to see in others. After this ritual, I met with the team in my office to discuss the climate and culture of the school, goals, and things they would like to do to promote school pride.

To further address the systemic issues impacting male students, I organized several "Project Save Our Boys" meetings. I invited guest speakers, community leaders, authors and men from the community to talk to students about responsible manhood and making positive choices. On this particular day, a young man joined the group. He was not a student at Rich South and he arrived alone. He was noticeably distraught. We were seated in a circle and were about to conclude the meeting. He sat down quietly to join us. It appeared that he was only there to listen. However, I focused my attention on him. I felt in my spirit that something was not right and that he was there for a greater cause.

When I asked him if there was anything he would like to share with the group he replied, "No." However, I pressed him, knowing that he wanted to get something off his chest. I told him that he was in a safe place to share with the group what was on his mind. To our surprise, he said that he was on his way to kill someone. He stunned the entire group, but everyone surprisingly remained calm. He said a few days ago his friend was murdered over a drug deal gone bad, and that he was on his way to avenge his death.

He said he heard about the meeting and decided to stop by. The young men in the group began talking to him about making the right choice and their experience with family members who have killed individuals and how it changed the trajectory of their lives. Parents also made an emotional plea for him to reconsider his plans. He began to get overwhelmed with emotion because he had more to lose than we expected. He said that he had a baby on the way. We stayed for hours talking to him.

We became his much-needed support network and voice of reason. I gave him a hug and my telephone number. I told him to call me whenever he needed to talk. I told him coming to the meeting was God's grace and mercy on his life. It was God's way of showing him that he had a greater plan for his life. I told him that the greater the struggle, the greater the success. He explained that the root cause of his anger was that his father was not present for much of his life. I told him that life is not fair, and that you have to play the cards you have been dealt. I gave him examples from my own life experience and told him to trust the process. When he left the meeting, his life would never be the same. He would have a chance to see the birth of his daughter. Also one year later he was married, had another child, and joined the Army. When he is in town, we talk about our chance encounter and how things could have turned out much differently. I make sure to tell him how proud I am of him, and how I hope he continues to make positive choices. He is an awesome family man and is doing quite well for himself. Encounters such as that one remind me that I'm working in the spirit of my divine purpose. I'm on assignment.

The girls' leadership team met every Thursday and was led by Associate Principal LaCour. She was God-fearing and was not to be taken lightly. They discussed in intimate details the aspects of their life. These conversations led to them becoming closer than ever before. Most of the young ladies felt that they suffered alone; however, they soon realized that they all shared similar experiences. For once they could be heard without being judged. Their sisterhood would translate into a significant reduction in physical altercations and in a positive culture and climate at the school.

Once considered "at risk," the young men and women in the mentoring programs were now leading the school. I like to refer to them as young men and women of promise. Their efforts resulted in a 90% reduction in physical altercations and a 70% reduction in tardies all within the first three months of the school year. My motto became: "You cannot teach a child you do not know, you do not love and you don't understand." I'm not afraid to tell my students that I love them. I always believed that establishing positive relationships and not overly testing students are the keys to raising academic achievement.

My first year at Rich South, I spent a lot of time with the boys and the girls always complained that I was not devoting an equal amount of time and attention to them. I never saw it from their perspective. However, in retrospect, they were absolutely right. Most of my time I gave to the boys, without considering how the girls felt. I made a public apology to them and came up with a plan to meet with them once a month on the weekend. Most of them saw me as a father figure and wanted my attention.

For our first meeting, I ordered whatever they wanted to eat: chicken, macaroni and cheese, string beans and cake. They didn't know it, but I also got roses for them at the conclusion of the meeting. Female staff members were also in attendance. Once the young ladies finished eating, we headed to the auditorium for an in-depth discussion. I knew the young ladies' desire to spend time with me was for a much greater cause and I was prepared to challenge them. We all sat on the stage in the auditorium. When I ask them why having my attention was so important to them, they gave superficial responses (i.e., "We just wanted to hang out," "You're cool," "We wanted to eat"). I responded to them in a more aggressive manner and said, "Stop playing with me… You and I both know that's not the reason why I'm here, now tell me the truth!"

The staff members were stunned; they didn't know what my angle was. The girls sat silently. I didn't utter a word and they became noticeably tense. One student started to rock back and forth in her seat and another buried her head in her lap. One of the girls mustered up enough courage to tell the story of how she was molested by her father. After, one by one, they began to tell their personal stories of how they were sexually molested at the hands of men that they trusted. They started crying. I was overwhelmed with emotion and wanted to protect the trust they had in me. I thought about my own daughter and how I would hurt a man if she was ever touched inappropriately. Many times, these girls were made to live in the house with the perpetrator because nobody believed them. I wanted to know first, if they were still living in an unsafe situation and second, how could I support them in moving forward.

They said that I made them feel safe and to keep doing what I was doing. They were relieved that they could tell their story without fear of judgment. Those young ladies had no idea of the steps I was prepared to take to keep them safe. They are true survivors. I was amazed at their strength. I was glad the female staff members were there to assist me. They became a source of strength to the girls as they too had survived, being victims of sexual abuse themselves. The girls traded numbers and I made sure they met with counselors to receive additional support. At the conclusion of the meeting, it was the perfect time to pass out the roses I bought for them earlier. It was truly a learning experience for me as their principal. When you put your hands on a man, you destroy an individual, but when you put your hands on a woman, you destroy a civilization.

I was invited to several Home Owners' Association (HOA) meetings and the common theme there was how unsafe the community was and how Rich South High School had become an embarrassment to the community. Students were fighting throughout the neighborhood and stealing at local stores. Most of these incidents took place after school. To address the matter, I started walking students to various locations in the neighborhood. While doing so, I introduced myself to the business owners. Being visible after school was nothing new for me because I've always walked with my students after school and gotten to know the nearby residents. This time would be no different.

Me walking after school to ensure my student made it home safely.
Me and security on the "Green Machine'

After several months of walking, District 227 purchased a John Deere motorized car we called "the Green Machine." Security started driving me around the neighborhood. This was a luxury because in the past I've always walked students everywhere. This form of transportation gave me an opportunity to expand my reach. I was seen all over the community. Rain, sleet or snow, I was outside every day. I took the safety of my students seriously; I also wanted to make a concerted effort to change the reputation that Rich South had in the community. Theft was always a problem at the local BP gas station on Sauk Trail in Richton Park. Students were stealing pop, chips, candy, and other goods. The BP gas station had cameras that captured still images of individuals stealing and they placed them at the front check-out line for patrons to see. When I arrived there after school one day, I noticed several pictures of my students stealing, and I was furious. I always warned my students of what I would do if they were ever caught stealing, and this was my opportunity to seize the moment.

I knew the students. The following day, I required the entire student body to come to the cafeteria. I told them that we had a thief amongst us and unless they came forward to pay retribution for what they had done, I would encourage staff and students to go to the BP gas station to see what a thief looks like. Immediately, the students ran to my office to come clean. I also had taken snapshots of the pictures on my cell phone. They were embarrassed about what they had done. I notified their parents and required them to pay back even more than what they had stolen. Once they fulfilled their obligation, I met with the store owners to have their pictures removed. After this happened a few times, incidents of theft involving Rich South students stopped completely.

The dramatic cultural shift at Rich South garnered national attention. It all started with a video that I posted on my Facebook page of an overweight student running on a treadmill, being encouraged by two of his peers that were running alongside him. The video averaged two million views a day and would end with over seventeen million views from people all over the world. I went from having a couple of friend requests to thousands upon thousands in the course of a week. My phone was ringing off the hook, people were calling the school and coming to visit and I had no idea who they were. Security had to be ramped up. It was a proud moment for the staff and students because for years Rich South had a bad reputation in the community and now we were evolving. We were on the Rachael Ray Show on Skype TV, in the newspapers, and on all of the local news networks in Chicago. However, the change did not come without criticism. I was accused of promoting prayers in school, which caused the Freedom From Religion Foundation to send letters to the District 227 office demanding my immediate termination in response. However, the Board President had studied me for years and knew of my potential. He knew where my heart lay and understood that with change comes resistance. I was fortunate; he was able to bear witness to a lot of things that I was doing and was able to communicate the actual facts to the Board of Education. He saw the changes as a "natural phenomenon," and kept me from

On Skype TV with me and students on the Rachel Ray Show.

Article written against me of Atheist group to have me terminated

facing possible termination. My mother always taught me that the, "[s]teps of a good man are ordered by the Lord," Psalms 37:23. I always put my trust in God and allow Him to guide my steps.

I love my students and tell them often how much I care about them; however, I am not afraid to hold them accountable. I have made recommendations to the superintendent to have students expelled because of choices they made that cause the school to be unsafe. I tell them that I am not responsible for their choices,

Principal Michael McGrone Sr.

Rich South PTSO

and that I will never compromise the safety of the whole for the actions of a few. I use natural and logical social consequences to teach them about the "real world." Though I'm known for using unconventional methods as an alternative to expulsions, safety is of the utmost importance. My favorite quote by Marva Collins is, "You have a right to fail, but you do not have a right to take teachers and other people with you."

The "new" Rich South caused a resurgence in the Parent Teacher Student Organization (PTSO). When Mr. Felker (the President) and Mrs. Williams (the Vice President) took over, they worked hard to revitalize the program. Years earlier, Mr. Felker was my own Academic Advisor at Governors State from 2009-11. I was denied from every school I applied to get my Master's Degree from in Educational Leadership; however, he took a chance on me and I got accepted. I was elated! He would play an important role in me graduating with my Master's Degree.

Here's where the story gets interesting. When I accepted the position as the Principal of Rich South in 2015, I ran into a student with the last name Felker. I said to myself, this couldn't be the kid whose father, years earlier, helped me earn my Master's Degree, so I asked where his father worked and he replied, "Governors State." I was floored! At that time, I knew that was his father. All along, he was preparing me to be responsible for his son's education. His son is a great kid. It was a pleasure helping him graduate as a member of the Class of 2017.

With Mr. Felker and Mrs. Williams' enthusiasm, they attracted other parents who became eager PTSO members and they would become a force to be reckoned with. They made t-shirts and attended school activities to make their presence known. They also met monthly to discuss ways they could support Rich South administrators to improve the culture and raise student achievement. They were a united front. Their ability to mobilize would be a life-altering experience for me when I made the decision to resign amid controversy at the District 227 main office. It was a stressful time because I was scheduled to undergo hip replacement surgery and the stress of everything was taking its toll on me, physically and mentally. I worked myself to exhaustion. At one point I had to leave work in a wheelchair because I was in so much pain that I couldn't walk. Because I went against the status quo, I was always in meetings at the district office. My thoughts were, "You cannot solve a problem with the same mentality that created it." The system in place was ineffective and I was focused on being creative! At times, I was written up for frivolous things. For example, the Superintendent once rushed to the building and falsely accused me of playing gospel music for students on "Turnup" Friday. I was furious and ended up arguing with a board member who was brought in to help resolve the issue. It felt as if despite my success, I was constantly being watched and questioned. I was placed on paid suspension for several days following that ordeal.

I was never a traditionalist. I worked outside the box. Having this philosophy cost me many jobs. When PTSO found out I had resigned, they knew there was more to the story than me simply walking away from responsibility. They were aware of the challenges going on at the district office and were determined to fight for my return. They made it loud and clear that they did not want me to leave and asked me to recall my resignation letter. After much prayer and thought, I wrote a letter rescinding my resignation. I never (in my career) had anyone fight for me. For once in my life I felt like I was understood.

The process to get reinstated would be more tumultuous than anyone could have ever expected. The board meetings were packed with PTSO members, community residents, staff and students. It was intense, and tempers flared. The board was split in their decision to have me reinstated; however, the community wanted me back and wanted their voices heard. Mrs. Felker and Mrs. Williams led the charge. They spoke with passion and conviction. Students also wrote letters expressing their desire for me to return. One by one, they spoke passionately about the impact I made in the school and in the community. One PTSO member went as far as to collect data she gathered from the police department to show how my presence significantly reduced incidents in the community as much as 40% in a two-year period. I had no idea of these numbers; however, she had the facts to prove it. All of the positive comments from students and the community left me in tears. I was truly overwhelmed by the show of support. Though it was a narrow margin (a 4-3 vote), the Board of Education voted to reinstate me. It was a joyous occasion. I was thankful for everyone's support, especially

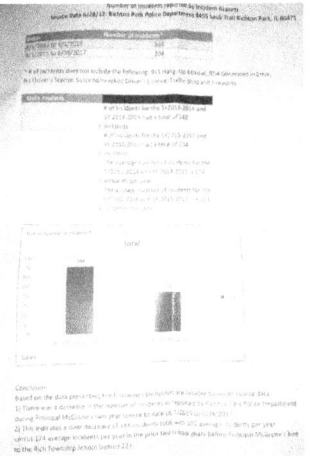

Data Parent research as a result of my presence in the community With PTSO after being Reinstated as Principal at Rich South H.S.

members of the PTSO who spearheaded it, sacrificing their time, energy and money to attend every single Board meeting.

However, the upcoming school year (2017-18) would bring even more unique challenges. The Board of Education voted unanimously to hire a permanent superintendent. Everyone was overjoyed because for years, the district had gone without a permanent superintendent. The new superintendent was considered a rising star in education and was given the red-carpet treatment. He would be responsible for getting the district out of the red and raising test scores. He shocked everyone when he announced that every administrator in the district would have to reapply for his or her job. He also said that he was restructuring the entire district. I knew right then that I would not be returning as the principal of Rich South High School because there were members of the Board who had voted against me, and this was their opportunity to have me removed. In my first meeting with the superintendent, he let me know that he received quite a few calls about me, some good, some bad; however, he wanted to get my side of the story. I told him that I was passionate about children and that I worked outside the box and it was not always perceived well by those in positions of power. I also spoke to him of the distrust I had with past leadership and that my experience with the district office was always negative. He said that he wanted to build a trusting relationship and I agreed with him. He said that if what I was doing was good for the kids, he wanted me to be on his team. I told him that we would work well together. I was hopefully optimistic.

In the first meeting the new superintendent had with Rich South's PTSO, he notified them of his plans to restructure the district and have all of the administrators reapply for their jobs. The PTSO members were concerned and were no fools. They didn't trust him and watched him closely.

The first week of the new school year, I complained to the superintendent that due to the turmoil over the summer I did not get a chance to hire an Associate Principal of Operations. I told him it would be very difficult to run the building with over a thousand students without an Associate Principal of Operations in place. However, my concerns fell upon deaf ears.

After complaining numerous times, I knew then that he had no intention on giving me the assistance I desperately needed. I told him I felt like I was being set up. I asked him if I could bring Mr. Gordan back (the former Associate of Principal of Operations and Buildings and Grounds, who had recently retired) and he agreed to it; however, this slight improvement still brought significant challenges because he could only work for 100 days out of the entire school year. In weeks following, a staff member approached me and ask me if I was aware I was being investigated for being in a "relationship" with a staff member and I responded, "No." When I contacted the superintendent to find out if he was aware of what was going on he responded, "Yes." When I asked him why didn't he alert me, being my direct supervisor, his response was that the Director of Human Resources should have notified me. I told him it was actions such as this that became the reason I had a distrust of the district office. That moment let me know that there would be a witch-hunt to terminate my employment.

When it came time for the principals to reapply for their jobs, I had no intentions on reapplying; however, Ms. LaCour convinced me to do so, even though I knew what the outcome would be. Over the years I'd grown to trust her and her instincts. She thought it was best that we continue what we started. The interview process was grueling. I interviewed a total of six different times. During each of the interviews, I stressed the importance of building relationships and social emotional learning. I reminded the Board that if we did not come up with strategic plans to address these issues, none of the new proposed initiatives would work. After the interviews were complete, my administrative team was confident that I was coming back; however, they would soon be hit with devastating news. On February 26th, 2018, the superintendent met with me in my office to explain the outcome of the interviews. He said that the decision was difficult, but

Principal Michael McGrone Sr.

that he was moving in another direction. I can honestly say that I wasn't shocked because the writing had been on the wall all along. He suggested that I meet with my administrative team to let them know the news. Upon doing so, Mrs. LaCour was in utter shock. She was speechless. Her eyes began to fill with tears.

As the news began to spread, it sent shockwaves throughout the Rich South H.S. community. Members of the PTSO and the community were livid and were prepared to fight once again. They rallied the troops. They picketed the district office, scheduled meetings and created flyers for the next Board meeting. Because the community was prepared to fight, I scheduled a private hearing (in closed session) with the Board of Education to plead my case. However, the superintendent was adamant about me not returning. He used a complex system to determine that I was not a "good fit" to be principal. The PTSO members who attended the private hearing explained to him that according to the Illinois School Report Card, my data in many cases exceeded other Rich Schools. For example, since my tenure, the number of students prepared for college went from 7% to 22%, which was more than double the usual rate. The superintendent stated that I would make a good "Associate Principal," at best. To defend my case I had two attorneys who agreed to represent me pro bono. They questioned his use of this "new system." Ultimately, it was the

Rich South flyer to garner my support

superintendent who made the final decision. What angered the parents even further was though I made the final cut I would not continue on as the principal of Rich South. Rich Central principal was rehired, and Rich East hired a new principal. Rich South would be the only school in the district without a principal.

I would be in the closed session for several hours and was exhausted. I finished my meeting with them at 8:30 P.M.; however, the Board of Education continued to deliberate until 1:30 A.M.

I was amazed at the persistence of the parents and students who stayed as long as they did. They were irritated because they felt the Board was trying to stall and get them to leave before they came up with the verdict. When they returned to the meeting, they voted 6 to 1 that I would be notified in writing of their decision. However, when I received the letter the following day, 6 board members voted to accept the superintendent's recommendation on not to rehire me and 1 voted against it. The letter stated that I could have a public hearing, which would be the last and final attempt for the board to reconsider my employment. Mrs. LaCour expressed her desire for me to keep fighting and I did. A special Board meeting was scheduled and I was the only one on the agenda. The meeting was packed and everyone (PTSO, students and the community) was prepared to speak on my behalf. I was asked to speak first. I focused my presentation on relationships (social and emotional learning) and how those were the single most important factors in "turning around" Rich South's reputation. This angered certain Board members and they let it be known how dissatisfied they were. They wanted me to talk about "data" and "test scores." The point I was trying to make was that so much emphasis is placed on "test scores" and "data" that we often forget about the development of the whole child. Nonetheless, the Board was not having it and stuck to their guns. After, one by one the Rich South community spoke passionately about the impact I made in the lives of students. They were emotional, and at times it got heated. One parent questioned the superintendent as to why he met with students at Rich South to tell them "negative things about Mr. McGrone." When he denied it, she brought her daughter to the stand to confirm what he had said. I was shocked that the superintendent would go through such great measures to question my integrity. Parents said that as elected officials, they expected the Board to vote favorably for me to be reinstated. Many of the community members felt that replacing me was a political move because it was obvious I was well-loved by the community and had some of the highest academic achievements in the district.

The board went into a closed session to deliberate. The meeting lasted for several hours. When they returned, they voted 5-2. By this time, the parents knew the outcome and were outraged. They screamed out, "Why don't you explain to the students what that means!" They began yelling and cursing at the Board members as they exited through the back door. It was the angriest I've ever seen the PTSO members. Students were crying and going off on the superintendent. I left the building quietly. I was stressed out and emotional, and I cried on the way home though I already knew the outcome. I was especially hurt for the students. Their voices were not heard. It finally hit me that after three years giving all that I had, my assignment was up. My goal was to end my career at Rich South; however, God had other plans. I like to say, "God doesn't play checkers, He plays chess." As time went on, the superintendent would dismantle my entire administrative team. For the 2018-19 school year, Rich South would have a completely new administrative staff. I was proud to work alongside my administrative team. They were experts of in their own right and together we change Rich South. Our Mantra: "We are the Best, the Brightest and the Boldest" will forever be etched in the stones of the great Rich South High School.

Throughout my career, I was always accused of being rebellious, combative, a renegade, etc. It is because I have never quite fit into a system where one size fits all. Education has often failed children, in particular, children of color, and I am not afraid to challenge the system. Because of low expectations, students of color are disproportionately expelled, they drop out of high school at higher rates than other students, or graduate despite being functionally illiterate and are ill-prepared for college and post-graduate careers. These students often end up on the streets, dead or in jail. These are far-reaching issues. Children today learn differently, and we have to adapt to the times. There's nothing more painful to hear educators say than that they have been teaching for years and years, as if that translates to students' achievement.

Are you current with the times? We as educators have to be revolutionary in our thought processes to challenge students to be global thinkers. This is the sole reason why I stress challenging staff to think "outside of the box." We are preparing students for things that don't yet exist. I've been called crazy and often referred to as "Joe Clarke" from the movie "Lean on Me" because of my unconventional tactics as an educator. I'm accustomed to doing whatever is necessary to keep students safe and ensure that they get the best possible instruction. I will make no apologies for that.

Rich Township District 227 is undergoing an evolution. Due to gentrification, more students of color are populating the school system as they continue to pour in from the city of Chicago. These students are bringing social economic challenges of epic proportions to District 227 and the Board of Education has the overwhelming responsibility of overhauling the Rich schools with qualified individuals who understand the demographics and who can move the district forward.

I'm grateful to be have been part of the Rich South District 227 family. I learned a great deal. Despite the challenges, I've grown as an administrator. Acknowledging that I work outside the box, I've been given the freedom to be creative. In doing so, my team and I made some extraordinary progress. My favorite quote by Vince Lombardi is, "The achievement of an organization are the combined efforts of each individual, those who work together will win". We put Rich South High School on a national stage.

Every now and again, you may hear me say, "I belong to the world." I mean that from the deepest depths of my soul. For the past 25 years, my work in education has been a culmination of comprehensive learning experiences, complex challenges, and great sacrifice. Through blood, sweat, and tears, I have been blessed to impact the lives of thousands of students, parents, and communities, through genuine relationship-building, social and emotional healing, and a strong determination to restore hope in those communities. The educational disparities we face are a national epidemic, and poverty and social dysfunction is a global pandemic. Knowing this, it is my deepest desire to go all over the nation, and all over the world, to help repair what is broken. Working with institutions of higher learning, school districts, parent organizations, social justice organizations, and social welfare agencies (to name just a few), will be critical in coming up with an all-inclusive strategy for healing and rebuilding. I saw education as being the first step in that journey, because I believe faith and education are at the nucleus of all change.

A renowned global entrepreneur once said that those who are crazy enough to think they can change the world are the ones that actually do. I like to think that they were considering me when they said that. It's easy for someone on the outside to look at urban neighborhoods and say, "This is unfixable." It's easy for someone to look at poverty-stricken communities and say, "This is a hopeless situation." It's easy for someone to look at the social, cultural, and political climate, and say to ourselves, "This is too much for us to take on."

As for me, I look at our current conditions, and I become inspired. It's not a story of hopelessness and failure; rather, our story is one of *hope*. To those who say that this work is too much to handle, I say that the race is not given to the strong, nor to the swift, but to those who endure until the end. No one said that this work would be easy, but we did say that it would be worthwhile. You have to believe it. You have to want it. You have to value it. Because the journey of a thousand steps starts with one. My reason for writing this book is to let people know that no matter what you go through in life it's possible.

About the Author

Principal Michael A. Mcgrone

Michael McGrone Sr. is the former principal at Rich South High School, located in Richton Park, Illinois. In his first year, Michael revolutionized the school, reducing physical altercations by 75 percent, and tardiness by 70 percent. In only two years, Michael increased college readiness from 7 percent to 22 percent. His work garnered national attention when the positive culture and climate of Rich South High School and Michael's boys' and girls' mentoring programs were highlighted on the Rachael Ray Show. He is an inspirational speaker and professional development consultant who regularly contracts with school districts, social service agencies, corporate and nonprofit agencies to help improve the experiences of students across the country.

A native of Gary, Indiana, Michael has sixteen brothers and sisters and a twin sister named Michelle. He has experienced many challenges throughout his life. Michael grew up during a time when Gary was being ravaged by drugs and violence. He lost friends to gun violence and was himself, a victim of the same, having once been held at gunpoint. Physically abused, failing third grade, graduating high school with a 1.2 GPA, and homeless his first year in college, Michael was enraged at the world and dissatisfied with the cards he was dealt. Yet he persevered, determined to attain greatness. He would eventually be the first African American in Bishop Noll's 88-year existence (a Catholic school located in Hammond, Indiana) to become Assistant Principal. He would also graduate with a 3.8 GPA, and his Master's in Educational Leadership from Governors State University.

Michael's love for children has evolved over a 25-year span working at numerous group homes, psychiatric facilities, and alternative, private, public and charter schools. The struggles he encountered in life gave him the tools necessary to motivate students to achieve their potential. His mentoring work with programs such as Men of Distinction, ACE Tech Ambassadors, and Men of Valor, has inspired the success of countless students. Michael is a renowned keynote speaker, willing to share his journey for the benefit of others. His innovative programs have been the catalyst for dramatic improvements wherever he has served children. Michael's unorthodox approach to education has drawn local and national attention. He has a unique way of inspiring others to

Principal Michael McGrone Sr.

strive for more by using his own life as an example that anything is possible. For speaking inquiries, programming, workshops, or consulting services, please visit www.PrincipalMcGrone.com.

www.ingramcontent.com/pod-product-compliance
Lightning Source LLC
Chambersburg PA
CBHW052030070526
44584CB00016B/1973